COURSE **3** **McDougal Littell Middle School**

Math

Larson   Boswell   Kanold   Stiff

Practice Workbook
Teacher's Edition

The Practice Workbook provides additional practice
for every lesson in the textbook. The workbook covers
essential vocabulary, skills, and problem solving. Space
is provided for students to show their work. The Teacher's
Edition includes the student workbook and the answers.

McDougal Littell
A HOUGHTON MIFFLIN COMPANY

Evanston, Illinois • Boston • Dallas

ISBN: 0-618-34362-8

123456789–BHV–07 06 05 04 03

Contents

Name _____ Date _____

Practice

1.1

For use with pages 5-9

In Exercises 1–3, use the graph at the right. It shows the typical cost of a college education at three types of colleges.

1. What type of graph is shown?

2. Which type of college is most expensive?

Which type of college is least expensive?

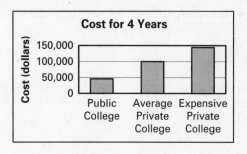

3. About how much would you expect to pay for an education at an average private college?

In Exercises 4–6, use the data below. It shows the number of hours worked by several employees in one week.

30, 48, 50, 42, 25, 40, 41, 48, 32, 35, 24, 20, 52, 48, 42, 46, 38, 32, 30, 27, 42, 41, 46, 45, 48, 32, 38, 39, 45, 59, 22, 25, 24, 48, 22, 45

4. Make a frequency table to organize the data using intervals of 5, starting with 20–24.

5. Make a histogram of the data displayed in the frequency table.

6. Which display would you use to make a quick visual comparison of the numbers of employees in the different intervals?

Name _____ Date _____

Practice

For use with pages 5–9

In Exercises 7–10, use the histogram below. It shows information about the weight of all the cats in a neighborhood.

7. About how many of the cats weigh 16–20.9 pounds?

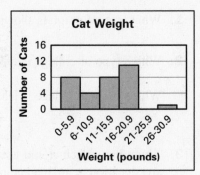

8. What two weight intervals have the same number of cats?

9. Are there more cats weighing *less than* 16 pounds or *at least* 16 pounds?

10. To show the numbers of neighborhood cats that are different colors, would a histogram be appropriate? Why or why not?

Name _____ Date _____

Practice

For use with pages 10–14

State the first step in evaluating the expression. Then evaluate it.

1. $12 - 3 \cdot 3$

2. $9 - 4 \div 2$

3. $\dfrac{16}{11 - 3}$

4. $6 \times 3 + (9 - 7)$

5. $5 \cdot \left[24 \div (5 + 3)\right] - 11$

6. $7 \times 8 + 63 \div 9$

In Exercises 7–15, evaluate the expression.

7. $8 \times 5 - 12$

8. $\dfrac{24}{9 - 5}$

9. $6 \times 8 - 7 \times 4$

10. $18 - 3 \times 5 + 2$

11. $(6 - 4) \times 5$

12. $\left[21 - (3 \cdot 7)\right] + 6$

13. $(18 - 6) \times 3 + 5$

14. $(20 \div 5) + (8 \times 7)$

15. $28 \div 4 \times (6 - 5)$

16. Samantha makes \$7 per hour mowing lawns and \$6 per hour cleaning a house. If she mows lawns for 5 hours and cleans for 9 hours, how much money does she earn? Use the expression $7 \times 5 + 6 \times 9$.

Lesson 1.2

Name _____ Date _____

Practice

For use with pages 10-14

In Exercises 17–25, evaluate the expression.

17. $\dfrac{2}{3} + \dfrac{4}{3} + \dfrac{6}{3}$

18. $15 \div \left[5 \times \left(\dfrac{1}{5} + \dfrac{2}{5} \right) \right]$

19. $12 \times \left(\dfrac{9}{6} + \dfrac{1}{6} \right)$

20. $(1.5 + 2.7) \times 8$

21. $3.6 \times (11 - 7)$

22. $9.2 - 4.8 \div 6$

23. $4 \times (11.3 - 8.7 + 1.6)$

24. $11.2 \div (24 - 17)$

25. $12 - (7.5 \div 15) \times 6$

26. A speeding ticket costs $100 plus $20 for each mile per hour over the speed limit the violator was traveling. Use the expression $100 + 8 \times 20$ to find the amount of a ticket for someone going 8 miles per hour faster than the speed limit.

27. During a basketball game, you make 6 two-point baskets and 3 three-point baskets. To find out how many points you scored for your team, evaluate the expression $2 \times 6 + 3 \times 3$.

28. Maria is making a dress that requires 3 yards of red ribbon and 2.5 yards of blue ribbon. She wants to make identical dresses for four of her friends. How much ribbon will she need for all of the dresses? Use the expression $3 \times 5 + 2.5 \times 5$.

Add parentheses to make the statement true.

29. $7 + 3 \times 4 - 1 = 39$

30. $3 \times 6 - 1 + 2 = 17$

31. $9 - 4 + 2 \times 7 = 49$

32. $6 - 3 \times 7 + 4 = 33$

LESSON 1.3 Practice

For use with pages 15–19

Tell whether the word or phrase suggests the operation of *addition*, *subtraction*, *multiplication*, or *division*.

1. more than

2. divided by

3. the product of

4. multiplied by

5. the difference of

6. increased by

7. the quotient of

8. fewer than

Evaluate the expression when $s = 5$ and $t = 9$.

9. $5s - 3$

10. $3t - 2s$

11. $\dfrac{4t}{s - 3}$

12. $\dfrac{7s + 1}{t - s}$

Evaluate the expression for the given values(s) of the variable(s).

13. $7m + 12$, when $m = 4$

14. $\dfrac{8p}{3}$ when $p = 6$

15. $7k - 3j$, when $k = 3$ and $j = 7$

16. $12h + 6i$, when $h = 6$ and $i = 5$

In Exercises 17–20, write the phrase as a variable expression. Let x represent the variable.

17. the total of 8 and a number

18. the quotient of a number and 3

19. 14 subtracted from a number

20. a number multiplied by 9

21. A triathlon event consists of 2.4 miles of swimming, 112 miles of biking, and 26.2 miles of running. Write a variable expression to find the number of miles a person travels in n triathlons. How far does a person travel in completing 4 triathlons?

22. The cost at a store for a package of pens is $3 and for a three-ring binder is $4. Write a variable expression for the cost of buying p packages of pens and b binders. How much would 3 packages of pens and 8 binders cost?

In Exercises 23–28, evaluate the expression when $x = 1.8$ and $y = 4$.

23. $3y - 4x$

24. $3xy$

25. $\dfrac{xy}{0.9}$

26. $7.5xy$

27. $8x - 3.2y$

28. $1.4y + 5.9x$

29. A car gets 21 miles per gallon of gasoline. There were g gallons of gasoline in the car when it started on a trip. The car has already gone 107 miles. Write a variable expression to find how many more miles the car can go. If the car had 6 gallons to start the trip, how much farther can the car go?

Name _____ Date _____

Practice

For use with pages 20–23

Match the vocabulary word with its description.

1. base

2. exponent

3. power

A. a product with a repeated factor

B. tells how many times a base is repeated

C. a repeated factor

Evaluate the power.

4. five cubed

5. nine squared

6. four to the fourth

7. 7^3

8. 11^2

9. 0^9

Write the product as a power and describe the power in words.

10. $4 \cdot 4 \cdot 4 \cdot 4 \cdot 4$

11. $12 \cdot 12$

12. $w \cdot w \cdot w$

Evaluate the expression.

13. $(9 - 7)^5 - 24$

14. $160 \div (11 - 7)^2$

15. $15 + (6 - 4)^8$

16. $5^2 + 4^3$

17. $(6 \times 9 - 40)^2 \div 49$

18. $421 - (11 + 9)^2$

In Exercises 19–21, evaluate the expression when $f = 7$.

19. $f^3 \div 7$

20. $(f - 2)^3 + 5$

21. $(2f)^2 - 105$

LESSON
1.4
Continued

Name _____ Date _____

Practice
For use with pages 20–23

22. A couple has four children. Each of those children have four children. Then each of those children have four children of their own. An expression for the number of great-grandchildren the original couple has is 4^3. How many great-grandchildren do they have?

23. A piece of gravel is kicked from the roof of a building, 240 feet above the ground. After t seconds, the piece of gravel has fallen $16t^2$ feet. How far from the ground is it after 3 seconds?

Complete the statement using <, >, or =.

24. 4^3____ 3^4

25. 6^2____ 5^2

26. 9^1____ 3^2

In Exercises 27–29, evaluate the expression when $x = 2.5$, $y = 8.1$, and $z = 12.3$.

27. $y^2 - x^2$

28. $4z^2 - 200$

29. $(z - y)^3$

30. The area of a square is given by the expression $s \cdot s$ square inches, where s is the length of a side in inches. Write the expression as a power. Then find the area of a square with a side length of 7 inches.

LESSON 1.5

Practice

For use with pages 26–31

Match the equation with the corresponding question.

1. $28 \div k = 7$

2. $7 + k = 28$

3. $\dfrac{k}{28} = 7$

4. $7k = 28$

A. What number divided by 28 is 7?

B. 28 divided by what number is 7?

C. The product of 7 and what number is 28?

D. What number added to 7 is 28?

Solve the equation using mental math.

5. $7x = 49$

6. $11 + m = 27$

7. $a - 7 = 13$

8. $\dfrac{20}{w} = 4$

9. $16 - k = 9$

10. $6g = 66$

11. $d + 23 = 35$

12. $26 - z = 19$

13. $\dfrac{t}{5} = 45$

Tell whether the value of the variable is a solution of the equation.

14. $x + 13 = 24; x = 11$

15. $6x = 54; x = 9$

16. $24 \div x = 12; x = 3$

17. $28 - x = 11; x = 7$

18. A group of six friends spent a total of $120 to purchase tickets to a concert. Use a verbal model to write and solve an equation to find what the cost of one ticket was.

19. An English teacher assigned a chapter of a book to read as homework. The chapter is 35 pages long. You were able to read 17 pages during class. Write an equation to find how many more pages you have to read as homework tonight. Then solve the equation.

Name _____ Date _____

1.5 Continued **Practice**
For use with pages 26–31

20. Explain how you would tell whether 7 is a solution of the equation $\frac{56}{x} = 8$.

21. Describe how you could use mental math to find the number of seconds in 20 minutes.

22. A car has been driven a total of 6000 miles. The owner has had the car for 3 months. Write and solve an equation to determine approximately how many miles the owner drives each month.

23. A woman deposited two checks at her bank for a total of $39. The amount of one check was $16. Write and solve an equation to determine the amount of the second check.

Name _____ Date _____

Practice

For use with pages 32–37

Find the perimeter and area of the rectangle or square.

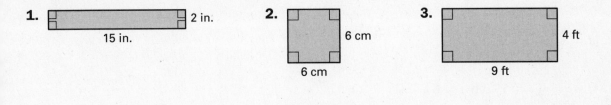

1. 15 in. | 2 in.

2. 6 cm | 6 cm

3. 9 ft | 4 ft

In Exercises 4–7, find the perimeter and area of the rectangle with the given measures.

4. length = 7 mm, width = 4 mm

5. length = 2 km, width = 6 km

6. length = 5 in., width = 11 in.

7. length = 13 yd, width = 8 yd

8. Find the side length of a square that has an area of 81 inches.

9. Find the side length of a square that has a perimeter of 12 yards.

10. The area of a rectangle is 60 square kilometers. The length is 12 kilometers. Use mental math to find the width of the rectangle.

Name _____ Date _____

Practice

For use with pages 32–37

Use the distance formula to find the missing value.

11. $d = 54$ miles, $r = 18$ mi/min, $t =$ _____

12. $d = 84$ in., $r =$ _____, $t = 7$ sec

13. $d =$ _____, $r = 55$ ft/h, $t = 6$ h

14. $d =$ _____, $r = 8.5$ cm/sec, $t = 11$ sec

15. A cheetah can run at a speed of 70 miles per hour (or 34.2 yards per second) for a distance of 200 yards. For how many seconds is the cheetah able to maintain this speed?

16. Claire is driving a car traveling at a steady speed of 63 miles per hour. She drives for 3 hours. How far does she drive?

17. The table shows information about the ground floors of two different houses. Complete the table.

	Length	Width	Area	Perimeter
House A	35 ft	30 ft		
House B	20 ft		1100 ft^2	

18. The world's fastest regular steam train, the *Cheltenham Flyer*, once traveled 77.3 miles at an average speed of 81.8 miles per hour. How long did the trip take?

Name _____ Date _____

Practice

For use with pages 38–43

1. It takes Robin 3 hours to mow the lawn and 1 hour to pull weeds in her garden. She does both four times a month. Use a problem solving plan to find how much time she spends on yard work in a month.

2. You use the Internet to purchase 9 tickets for a concert. The tickets are $22 each. You have to pay a handling fee of $3 per ticket and a shipping fee of $5 for the entire order. Use a problem solving plan to find your total cost.

3. You make a long distance phone call to a friend that lasts 28 minutes. The long distance company charges you $.99 for the first two minutes of the call and $.10 for each minute after the first two. How much does the call cost you?

4. A recipe for tomato and pasta salad calls for 32 ounces of canned tomatoes and 4 cups of cooked macaroni. The recipe makes 8 servings. You only want to make enough for 2 servings. What amounts of canned tomatoes and macaroni should you use?

In Exercises 5–8, complete the pattern.

5. 6, 13, 20, ____, ____

6. 81, 27, 9, ____, ____

7. 16, 13, 10, ____, ____

8. 1, 8, 64, ____, ____

9. The product of two numbers is 36. Their sum is 13. Find the two numbers.

Name _____ Date _____

Practice

For use with pages 38–43

10. A travel agency has a goal to sell 10,500 airline tickets in a business week. On Monday the agency sells 3269 tickets, on Tuesday the agency sells 2004 tickets, and on Wednesday the agency sells 2807 tickets. How many tickets does the agency still need to sell on Thursday and Friday to meet its goal?

11. A local newspaper held an open house for students in the town's four middle schools to come and see how newspapers are made. There were 126 girls at the open house from Central Middle School, 87 girls from East Middle School, 114 girls from West Middle School, and 216 girls from Hillside Middle School. The total number of boys that attended was 26 less than the total number of girls. How many students attended in all?

Complete the pattern.

12. $3x, 9x, 27x,$ ____, ____

13. $4x^2, 10x^2, 16x^2,$ ____, ____

14. $67x, 55x, 43x,$ ____, ____

15. $19x, 22x^2, 25x^3, 28x^4,$ ____, ____

Name _____ Date _____

Practice

For use with pages 53–56

Does the given arrow show the location of the *positive* integers or the *negative* integers?

1. A

2. B

Order the integers from least to greatest.

3. $17, -24, -16, -8, 7, 2, 23$

4. $-16, -24, -38, 25, 11, -56, 102, -136$

5. $-7, -5, 2, -1, 4, 6, -10, 0$

6. $8, -15, 17, -39, -51, 73, -84$

Write the opposite and the absolute value of the integer.

7. 7

8. -25

9. 106

10. -241

Complete the statement with < or >.

11. -6 ____ 4

12. -2 ____ -4

13. 0 ____ 8

14. -11 ____ -3

15. 31 ____ -16

16. -24 ____ -28

Match the integer expression with the verbal expression.

17. $-|12|$

18. $|-12|$

19. $-|-12|$

20. $-(-12)$

21. $|12|$

A. the opposite of negative twelve

B. the absolute value of twelve

C. the opposite of the absolute value of negative twelve

D. the absolute value of negative twelve

E. the opposite of the absolute value of twelve

Practice

For use with pages 53–56

Simplify the expression.

22. $|-15|$ **23.** $-(-9)$ **24.** $|-16|$

25. $-|-6|$ **26.** $-(-|49|)$ **27.** $-[-(-34)]$

In Exercises 28–30, use the table at the right. It shows the distances of the runners from the finish line when the winner won the race.

28. Who won the race?

29. Who finished farther back, Sara or Tamika?

30. Arrange the girls' names in order from first-place to last-place finish.

Runner	Distance (ft)
Sarah	-16
Beth	-2
Juanita	0
Tamika	-9
Ingrid	-36

Lesson 2.1

Name _____ Date _____

Practice

For use with pages 57-62

1. What addition problem does the number line show? What is the sum?

Use a number line to find the sum.

2. $5 + (-4)$

3. $-8 + 3$

4. $-2 + (-7)$

Find the sum.

5. $-54 + 63$

6. $29 + (-46)$

7. $-38 + (-59)$

8. $-93 + 86$

9. $12 + 38 + (-41)$

10. $-28 + 31 + (-44)$

11. $-101 + 95 + (-37)$

12. $53 + (-19) + (-102)$

13. $-98 + (-91) + 68$

Complete the statement using *always, sometimes,* or *never.*

14. The sum of two positive integers is _____ zero.

15. The sum of zero and a positive integer is _____ zero.

16. The sum of zero and a negative integer is _____ zero.

17. The sum of a positive integer and a negative integer is _____ zero.

In Exercises 18–21, find the sum.

18. $38 + 51 + (-29) + (-73)$

19. $-34 + (-85) + 63 + 47$

20. $102 + (-173) + 226 + (-185)$

21. $-304 + 246 + (-189) + 107$

Name _____ Date _____

Practice

For use with pages 57-62

22. Steven's bank account balance was $212 at the beginning of the month. He
withdrew $63, $74, and $39. He also deposited $105 and $86. What was
his balance after these transactions?

23. Yolanda was 8 seconds behind the leader after one lap of a two-mile track
race. The same person led the race the whole way and won it. Here is how
Yolanda lost or gained time on the leader in each of the remaining laps:
lost 9 seconds, lost 3 seconds, gained 1 second, gained 2 seconds, gained
5 seconds, lost 3 seconds, gained 13 seconds. How many seconds behind
the leader did Yolanda finish?

Name _____ Date _____

Practice

For use with pages 63–67

Find the difference.

1. $7 - 11$

2. $-6 - 9$

3. $-5 - (-12)$

4. $-13 - 8$

5. $-16 - (-11)$

6. $15 - 18$

7. $23 - (-17)$

8. $21 - 35$

9. $-34 - (-18)$

10. $46 - 57$

11. $-61 - (-49)$

12. $-37 - 58$

Translate the verbal phrase into a numerical expression and solve.

13. The difference of a negative six and nineteen

14. The difference of eight and negative twenty-one

15. The difference of the opposite of fifteen and the opposite of twenty-eight

Evaluate the expression when $x = -8$ and $y = 5$.

16. $7 - x - y$

17. $x - 15 - y$

18. $x - y - 4 - 12$

19. Jose's credit card statement says that he owes $324. He charges an additional $63, $21, and $75. How much does he owe now?

20. A scuba diver is 31 feet below the surface of the water. She dives down an additional 16 feet. How far would she have to rise to reach the surface of the water?

Name _____ Date _____

Practice

For use with pages 63–67

Evaluate the expression.

21. $57 - 304$

22. $-568 + 493$

23. $-219 - (-1065)$

24. $-8 - (-4) - (-7)$

25. $-16 - 10 - (-14)$

26. $63 - 48 - 39$

27. $-34 - (-15) - (-18)$

28. $37 - (-41) - 86$

29. $-54 - 81 - (-47)$

Evaluate the expression when $a = -5$, $b = 12$, and $c = -8$.

30. $a - b - 14$

31. $b - c + a$

32. $b - 11 - c$

33. $c - 7 - a$

34. $c - 16 + b$

35. $a - b - c$

36. Which of the temperature changes represents the greatest temperature drop in degrees?

    a. From 16°F down to −21°F

    b. From −4°F down to −39°F

    c. From 33°F down to −6°F

    d. From −14°F down to −54°F

37. The values below show the daily change (in cents) in the value of one share of stock.

    $-17, -7, +3, -8, +12, -21, -33, +34, -11, -19$

    What was the total change in the value of the stock over the 10 days?

Lesson 2.3

Name _____ Date _____

Practice
For use with pages 68–73

Find the product.

1. $4(-9)$

2. $-5(-7)$

3. $-12(0)$

4. $-9(-11)$

5. $-12(8)$

6. $-13(-20)$

7. $-17(18)$

8. $-4(-9)(8)$

9. $6(-5)(7)$

10. $-9(-8)(11)$

11. $42(-3)(0)$

12. $-5(-7)(-13)$

Evaluate the expression when $x = -9$, $y = -7$, and $z = -11$.

13. $2xy$

14. $-6yz$

15. $yz - 4x$

16. $xy + 3z$

17. $7xyz$

18. $5xy - 7zx$

Find the product.

19. $|-12| \cdot 4$

20. $-7 \cdot |9|$

21. $-4(-8) \cdot |-5|$

In Exercises 22–24, use mental math to solve the equation.

22. $3x = -21$

23. $-12x = -36$

24. $-3(5)x = 75$

Name _____ Date _____

Practice
For use with pages 68–73

25. A roofing contractor has 29 bundles of roofing shingles that he needs to carry up a ladder and put onto a roof. He carries two bundles at a time. How many bundles are still on the ground after his seventh trip up the ladder?

26. A football team starts with the ball at their own 20-yard line. They make two 6-yard gains in a row, then they have three 5-yard losses in a row. What yard line is the ball on at this point?

In Exercises 27–29, evaluate the expression when $x = -6$ and $y = -13$.

27. $-x(y)$ **28.** $x(y^2)(x)$ **29.** $[y + (-x)(y)]^2$

30. There is an old saying that goes, "Every time I go one step forward, I get bumped two steps backward." Taken literally, what would the person's forward progress be after going through this process 23 times?

31. You went to the department store for back to school shopping and picked out 6 shirts and 4 pairs of pants with a total worth of $170. When you paid for the clothes, the cashier took $3 off the price of each shirt and $5 off the price of each pair of pants. There was no sales tax. How much did you have to pay?

Lesson 2.4

Name _____ Date _____

Practice

For use with pages 74–77

Find the quotient.

1. $\dfrac{-64}{-8}$

2. $\dfrac{-32}{4}$

3. $\dfrac{50}{-10}$

4. $\dfrac{0}{-29}$

5. $\dfrac{-65}{0}$

6. $\dfrac{-36}{3}$

7. $\dfrac{30}{-15}$

8. $\dfrac{56}{-7}$

9. $\dfrac{-36}{4}$

10. $\dfrac{-48}{-6}$

11. $\dfrac{42}{-2}$

12. $\dfrac{-60}{-12}$

Evaluate the expression when $a = -24$, $b = -6$, and $c = -12$.

13. $\dfrac{a}{b}$

14. $\dfrac{bc}{a}$

15. $\dfrac{-c}{b}$

16. $\dfrac{ac}{b}$

17. $\dfrac{c^2}{a}$

18. $\dfrac{(a + c)}{b}$

Find the mean of the data.

19. $8, 5, -4, 9, -3, 11, 2$

20. $-7, -13, 5, 2, -8, -9$

21. $-16, 2, -18, 4, -11, -8, -6, 5$

22. $-4, 11, -6, 14, -3, 7, 2$

Name _____ Date _____

Practice

For use with pages 74–77

Use the table at the right, showing the final golf scores, relative to par, of the top eleven golfers at the 2001 Masters Tournament.

Player	Final
T. Woods	−12
R. Goosen	−9
P. Mickelson	−8
J. Olazabal	−7
P. Harrington	−6
E. Els	−6
V. Singh	−5
S. Garcia	−4
M. Jimenez	−3
A. Scott	−3
A. Cabrera	−3

23. Calculate the mean score of the golfers.

24. Par for the tournament was 288 strokes. Find the actual number of strokes taken by each of the golfers. For example, to find Tiger Woods's number of strokes, subtract 288 − 12. So, Woods took 276 strokes in the tournament.

25. What is the *mean* number of strokes taken in the tournament by the 11 golfers?

26. Convert the average score against par found in Exercise 23 to a number of strokes. How does the number compare with the average you found in Exercise 25?

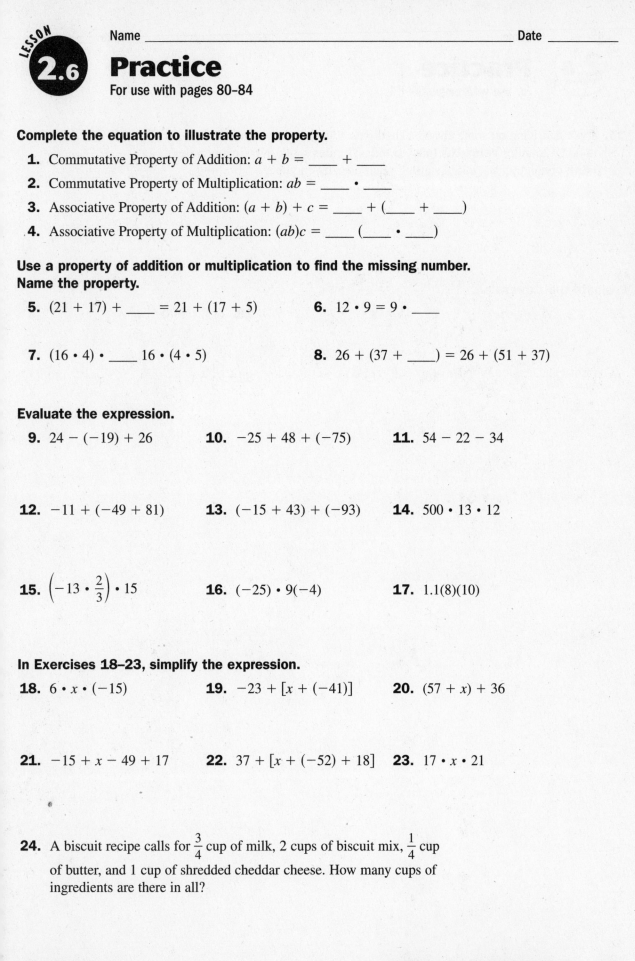

LESSON 2.6

Practice
For use with pages 80–84

Complete the equation to illustrate the property.

1. Commutative Property of Addition: $a + b =$ ____ + ____

2. Commutative Property of Multiplication: $ab =$ ____ • ____

3. Associative Property of Addition: $(a + b) + c =$ ____ + (____ + ____)

4. Associative Property of Multiplication: $(ab)c =$ ____ (____ • ____)

Use a property of addition or multiplication to find the missing number. Name the property.

5. $(21 + 17) +$ ____ $= 21 + (17 + 5)$ **6.** $12 • 9 = 9 •$ ____

7. $(16 • 4) •$ ____ $16 • (4 • 5)$ **8.** $26 + (37 +$ ____$) = 26 + (51 + 37)$

Evaluate the expression.

9. $24 - (-19) + 26$ **10.** $-25 + 48 + (-75)$ **11.** $54 - 22 - 34$

12. $-11 + (-49 + 81)$ **13.** $(-15 + 43) + (-93)$ **14.** $500 • 13 • 12$

15. $\left(-13 • \dfrac{2}{3}\right) • 15$ **16.** $(-25) • 9(-4)$ **17.** $1.1(8)(10)$

In Exercises 18–23, simplify the expression.

18. $6 • x • (-15)$ **19.** $-23 + [x + (-41)]$ **20.** $(57 + x) + 36$

21. $-15 + x - 49 + 17$ **22.** $37 + [x + (-52) + 18]$ **23.** $17 • x • 21$

24. A biscuit recipe calls for $\dfrac{3}{4}$ cup of milk, 2 cups of biscuit mix, $\dfrac{1}{4}$ cup of butter, and 1 cup of shredded cheddar cheese. How many cups of ingredients are there in all?

Name _____ Date _____

Practice
For use with pages 80-84

25. Ryan is driving on some errands. He drives 17 miles north. Then he drives another 26 miles north. His final errand is 7 miles south. How many miles north or south of his initial starting point does he end up?

Evaluate the expression.

26. $7.4 + 3.5 + (-5.4)$

27. $15 \cdot (8 \cdot 2 \cdot 3)$

28. $6(3 \times 9)(0.5)$

29. $\left(\frac{4}{5} + 2\right) - \frac{2}{5}$

30. $-\frac{1}{3} \cdot 13 \cdot 15$

31. $\left(\frac{3}{8} \cdot 11\right) \cdot 16$

Lesson 2.6

Name _____ Date _____

Practice

For use with pages 85–90

Use the distributive property to write an equivalent expression.

1. $-5(y + 7)$

2. $4(11 + 6)$

3. $6(8 + m)$

4. $-31(24 + 12)$

5. $13[7 + w + (-9)]$

6. $-29(p - 21 - 5)$

Simplify the expression by combining like terms.

7. $c + 8c + 5d$

8. $4m + 3k + 6m + 9k$

9. $8s + 6t - (-5s) - 2t$

10. $15c + 12d - 7d - 3c$

11. $-16g + 3h - 19h - 4g$

12. $8x + 5y + 11x - 2y$

Find the total area of the two rectangles.

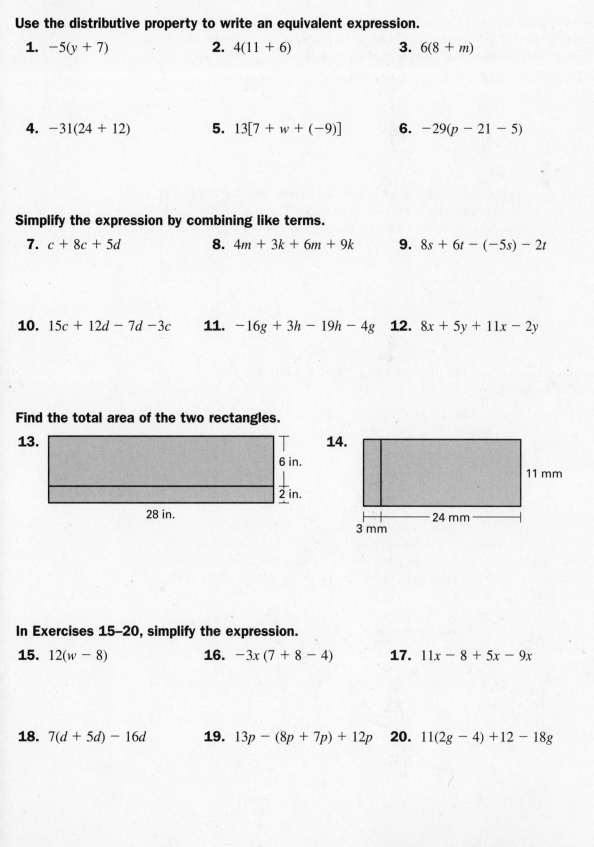

13.

6 in.

2 in.

28 in.

14.

11 mm

3 mm

24 mm

In Exercises 15–20, simplify the expression.

15. $12(w - 8)$

16. $-3x (7 + 8 - 4)$

17. $11x - 8 + 5x - 9x$

18. $7(d + 5d) - 16d$

19. $13p - (8p + 7p) + 12p$

20. $11(2g - 4) + 12 - 18g$

Name _____ Date _____

Practice

For use with pages 85–90

21. A bride is buying gifts for the seven attendants in her bridal party. She wants to get each a necklace for $21.85 and a pair of earrings for $8.15. Explain how to use mental math to find how much money she will need for these gifts.

22. Maria wants to put tint on windows that have the dimensions shown at the right. The material for the tint costs $1.99 a square foot. How much will it cost to buy enough material for both windows?

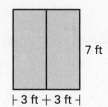

7 ft

⊦ 3 ft ⊦ 3 ft ⊣

In Exercises 23–26, find the product using mental math and the distributive property.

23. 7(15)   **24.** 4(23)   **25.** 12(18)   **26.** 30(52)

27. A company is putting vinyl siding up across the back of two condominium units. Both units are 15 feet high. One unit is 27 feet wide and the other is 31 feet wide. Write an expression for the area of siding needed. Then find the amount.

Lesson 2.7

LESSON 2.8

Name _____ Date _____

Practice

For use with pages 91–95

Give the coordinates of the point.

1. A

2. D

3. B

4. E

5. C

6. F

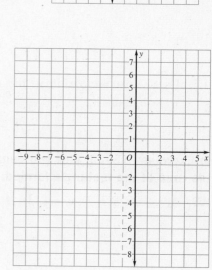

Plot the point in a coordinate plane and describe its location.

7. $(-5, 3)$

8. $(1, -4)$

9. $(0, -1)$

10. $(3, 7)$

11. $(-6, 0)$

12. $(-8, -5)$

Plot and connect the given points. Then identify the resulting figure and find its perimeter.

13. $(-1, 0), (-1, 4), (-4, 4), (-4, 0)$

14. $(3, -5), (3, 3), (-2, 3), (-2, -5)$

15. $(-6, -3), (-6, 2), (-1, 2), (-1, -3)$

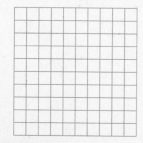

Lesson 2.8

2.8 Continued **Practice**
For use with pages 91–95

In Exercises 16–17, use the ordered pairs below that give data for the amount of money you earn at a new job. The *x*-coordinate represents the number of hours you work and the *y*-coordinate represents the amount of money you earn.

(1, $8.50), (2, $17.00), (3, $25.50), (4, $34.00)

16. Plot the points in a coordinate plane. Identify the pattern.

17. Use the pattern to estimate the amount of money you would earn if you work 6 hours.

In Exercises 18–20, plot and connect the points. Find the perimeter and the area of the rectangle formed.

18. $A(7, -2), B(7, 3), C(-1, 3), D(-1, -2)$

19. $W(-5, 6), X(2, 6), Y(2, 0), Z(-5, 0)$

20. $J(0, 0), K(0, -5), L(-6, -5), M(-6, 0)$

Lesson 2.8

Name _____ Date _____

Practice
For use with pages 107–112

Solve the equation.

1. $x + 7 = 9$

2. $w - 11 = 12$

3. $13 + z = 6$

4. $l - 8 = 23$

5. $42 = a - 26$

6. $36 = w + 19$

7. $26 + m = 14$

8. $z - 9 = 8$

9. $36 = b + 16$

10. $40 = z - 12$

11. $28 = d - 23$

12. $m + 35 = 41$

In Exercises 13–16, tell whether the equation correctly represents the real-life problem. If not, correct the equation.

13. You are 3 inches taller than you were last year. Last year you were 60 inches tall. How tall are you now? Equation: $60 = h - 3$

14. A prime rib dinner at a restaurant costs $21.95. A chicken dinner at the same restaurant is $7 cheaper. What is the cost of a chicken dinner? Equation: $c - 7 = 21.95$

15. At last week's football game there were 125 people in attendance. This week there were 34 more people. How many people attended the football game this week? Equation: $125 = p + 34$

16. The trip from West Lafayette, Indiana, to Chicago, Illinois, takes $2\frac{1}{4}$ hours. The trip from Ann Arbor, Michigan, to Erie, Pennsylvania, takes $2\frac{1}{2}$ hours longer to drive. How long does it take to drive from Ann Arbor to Erie? Equation: $2\frac{1}{2} + d = 2\frac{1}{4}$

Name _____ Date _____

Practice
For use with pages 107–112

17. Write a word problem that can be represented by the equation
$x + 13 = 25$.

Solve the equation.

18. $x + \dfrac{2}{3} = \dfrac{2}{3}$

19. $w - \dfrac{1}{8} = \dfrac{9}{8}$

20. $m + 6.4 = 9.8$

21. $8.15 + p = 11.39$

22. $q + \dfrac{1}{5} = \dfrac{3}{5}$

23. $y - 1.056 = 2.981$

24. The drive from Las Vegas, Nevada, to Los Angeles, California, is 275 miles. Your family has already driven 132 miles of the trip. How much farther do you have to drive to reach Los Angeles? Write a verbal model. Then write and solve an algebraic model for the problem.

LESSON 3.2 Practice

For use with pages 113–116

Complete the solution. Justify each step.

1. $7x = 35$

$$\frac{7x}{\_\_} = \frac{35}{\_\_}$$

$$x = \_\_$$

2. $\dfrac{r}{2} = -24$

$$\frac{r}{2} \cdot \_\_ = -24 \cdot \_\_$$

$$r = \_\_$$

Solve the equation. Check your solution.

3. $\dfrac{w}{4} = 16$

4. $7 = \dfrac{k}{8}$

5. $\dfrac{q}{3} = 10$

6. $6x = 48$

7. $66 = 11m$

8. $14g = 98$

9. $\dfrac{y}{16} = 6$

10. $\dfrac{h}{20} = 13$

11. $22 = \dfrac{d}{17}$

12. $13f = 195$

13. $204 = 51x$

14. $34a = 272$

15. You babysat for 8 hours one night and earned $64. Which equation can you use to find how much you earned in 1 hour?

A. $64b = 8$
B. $8b = 64$
C. $\dfrac{b}{8} = 64$
D. $b = \dfrac{8}{64}$

Describe an inverse operation that will undo the given operation.

16. Multiplying by 9

17. Dividing by -6

18. Adding -11

Lesson 3.2

LESSON

3.2
Continued

Practice

For use with pages 113–116

Solve the equation. Check your solution.

19. $\dfrac{x}{3} = -12$

20. $26 = -2d$

21. $-7m = -119$

22. $8 = \dfrac{z}{1.9}$

23. $\dfrac{c}{13} = -2.01$

24. $54 = 0.9y$

25. $-1.8t = 27$

26. $\dfrac{v}{6.3} = -7$

27. $-45 = -0.5b$

28. $527u = 2108$

29. $27 = \dfrac{-a}{4.3}$

30. $34 = -1.7s$

31. Tickets to a concert are \$32 each. Five friends want to purchase their tickets together. What is the total price for the tickets?

Lesson 3.2

Name _____ Date _____

Practice

For use with pages 117–123

Solve the equation.

1. $7x + 3 = 31$

2. $5t - 9 = 26$

3. $8 + 6m = 26$

4. $4 + 12r = 112$

5. $-3z - 7 = 23$

6. $36 = 8 - 14p$

7. $63 = 3x + 9$

8. $28 = 16 - 4m$

9. $7h - 15 = 48$

10. $124 - 8g = 36$

11. $13b - 76 = 28$

12. $15m + 26 = 236$

13. To find the number of pints in 3 quarts and 2 pints, you can evaluate the expression $3(2) + 2$. You have 2 gallons and 1 pint of milk in your refrigerator. Write and evaluate an expression that will give you the amount of milk, in pints, in your refrigerator. (*Hint*: 1 gallon = 4 quarts)

14. At the grocery store, you bought 4 boxes of cereal and a carton of strawberries. The carton of strawberries costs $2.89. The bill came to a total of $12.25. How much was one box of cereal?

Solve the equation. Check your answer.

15. $6m + 15 = 12$

16. $\frac{x}{4} - 7 = 9$

17. $-6 + \frac{f}{3} = 2$

18. $13 = 5 + \frac{g}{9}$

19. $7 + \frac{d}{6} = 19$

20. $11 - c = 18$

21. $4 = 25 - 7y$

22. $34 - 7q = -8$

23. $67 = 13 + \frac{u}{9}$

24. $-94 = 25 + \frac{a}{7}$

25. $19 - 4z = -5$

26. $\frac{k}{8} - 37 = -5$

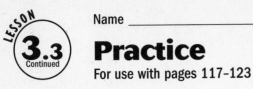

Practice

For use with pages 117-123

27. Shannon gets $12 for every lawn she mows. One day she received $5 in tips. If she earned a total of $101 that day, how many lawns did she mow?

28. Tickets to a concert are $24 apiece. There is also a $5 handling fee for the entire order. You and some friends ordered tickets and the bill came to a total of $173. How many tickets did you order?

Solve the equation.

29. $4(m + 1) = 8$

30. $7 = -1(q + 13)$

31. $8\left(\dfrac{1}{4} + x\right) = 18$

Name _____ Date _____

Practice
For use with pages 124–129

1. A restaurant charges you $.15 for every drink refill that you order. The cost of your dinner is $14. Which equation can you use to find the number of drink refills you ordered if your bill came to $14.60?

   A. $14w + 0.15 = 14.60$ **B.** $14 + 0.15w = 14.60$

   C. $0.15 + w + 14 = 14.60$

In Exercises 2 and 3, translate the statement into an equation. Then solve the equation.

2. The difference of 8 and the quotient of a number and 6 is 9.

3. The product of a number increased by 10 and 4 is 22.

4. Diane is taking a trip that is 224 miles long. She has already driven 59 miles. If she drives at a speed of 55 miles per hour, how many more hours will she need to drive to reach her destination?

5. Together, David and Carol have a total of 35,000 frequent flyer miles with an airline. Carol has 19,000 miles. After going on a business trip, David has 1200 more miles than he had last month. How many frequent flyer miles did David have last month?

6. Write a word problem that can be modeled by the equation $\frac{x}{4} + 8 = 10$.

7. Jessica is printing invitations to a graduation party. She needs to print 250 invitations, one per sheet of paper. She was only able to purchase 5 packages of 25 sheets of paper at the store. How many more packages of paper does she need in order to print the rest of the invitations?

Name _____ Date _____

Practice
For use with pages 124–129

In Exercises 8–14, translate the statement into an equation. Then solve the equation.

8. A number times 7, increased by 3, is 59.

9. The difference of the product of 4 times a number and $\frac{2}{3}$ is $\frac{34}{3}$.

10. 24 decreased by the quotient of a number and 6 is -5.

11. 9.8 increased by the quotient of a number and 5 is 10.4.

12. The product of 4 and a number divided by 7 is 24.

13. The quotient of -54 and 9, subtracted from 8 times a number, is -18.

14. The product of a number and 6 squared divided by 4 is 117.

Name _____ Date _____

LESSON
3.5 **Practice**
For use with pages 132–139

Find the area and the perimeter of the triangle.

1.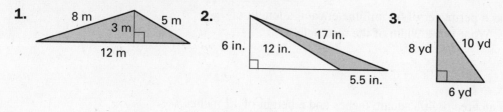

8 m   3 m   5 m
12 m

2.

17 in.
6 in. 12 in.
5.5 in.

3.

8 yd   10 yd
6 yd

Find the value of the variable.

4. $A = 144 \text{ yd}^2$

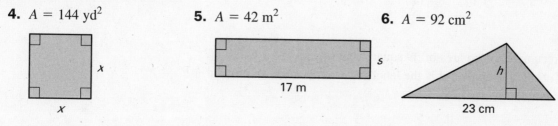

x
x

5. $A = 42 \text{ m}^2$

s
17 m

6. $A = 92 \text{ cm}^2$

h
23 cm

Find the value of the variable.

7. $P = 38 \text{ mm}$

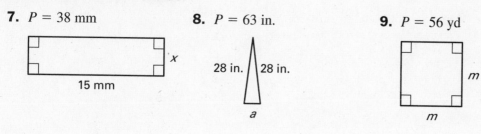

x
15 mm

8. $P = 63 \text{ in.}$

28 in. 28 in.
a

9. $P = 56 \text{ yd}$

m
m

Name _____ Date _____

Practice

For use with pages 132–139

Find the length of each side.

10. A rectangle has a perimeter of 64 millimeters and a length of 19 millimeters. What is the width of the rectangle?

11. A triangle has an area of 408 square inches and a height of 17 inches. What is the length of its base?

12. A triangle has an area of 37 square feet and a base with a length 8.4x feet. What is the height of the triangle in terms of x?

13. A rectangle has an area of 39 square centimeters and a width of 8.1w centimeters. What is the length of the rectangle in terms of w?

Find the area of the shaded region in the figure.

14.

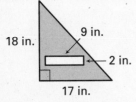

18 in. 9 in. 2 in. 17 in.

15.

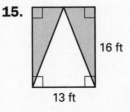

16 ft 13 ft

40   **Middle School Math, Course 3**
Chapter 3   Practice Workbook

Name _____ Date _____

Practice

For use with pages 140–145

Match the inequality with its graph.

1. $x < 8$

2. $x \geq -8$

3. $x \leq -8$

4. $x > 8$

A. ◄─┼─┼─┼─┼─┼─┼─┼─○─►
    −8 −6 −4 −2 0 2 4 6 8

B. ◄─┼─┼─┼─┼─┼─┼─┼─○─►
    −8 −6 −4 −2 0 2 4 6 8

C. ◄●─┼─┼─┼─┼─┼─┼─┼─►
    −8 −6 −4 −2 0 2 4 6 8

D. ◄●─┼─┼─┼─┼─┼─┼─┼─►
    −8 −6 −4 −2 0 2 4 6 8

Write a verbal phrase to describe the inequality.

5. $f \geq -4$ **6.** $d < 9$ **7.** $w > -19$ **8.** $g \leq 0$

Solve the inequality. Then graph its solution.

9. $x + 8 > 9$ **10.** $10 \geq m - 3$ **11.** $p + 4 < 2$

12. $13 > 5 + f$ **13.** $7 \leq a - 9$ **14.** $6 + y > 4$

15. $q + 8 \geq -5$ **16.** $-29 + v \leq -51$ **17.** $-32 > j - 29$

18. $-2.8 < k - 7.0$ **19.** $m + \frac{1}{3} > 4$ **20.** $t - 4.6 < 5.9$

Name _____ Date _____

Practice

For use with pages 140–145

Tell whether the number is a solution of the inequality graphed below.

<-----+---+---●---+---+---+---+---+---+---+---+---+---+----->
   -7 -6 -5 -4 -3 -2 -1 0 1 2 3 4 5

21. -6.5 **22.** 0 **23.** $-3\frac{1}{2}$ **24.** 4

In Exercises 25 and 26, use the following information. You are trying to run 5 miles in less than 30 minutes. You run the first mile in 5 minutes, the second mile in 7 minutes, the third mile in 8 minutes, and the fourth mile in 6 minutes.

25. Write and solve an inequality that represents the time in which you must run the last mile in order to run 5 miles in less than 30 minutes.

26. Graph the range of the times for the last mile.

Write a verbal sentence that describes the compound inequality.

27. $-3 < x < 4$ **28.** $8 \le h \le 13$ **29.** $0 < w \le 7$

Name _____ Date _____

Practice

For use with pages 146–149

Solve the inequality. Then graph its solution.

1. $\frac{1}{6}m > 2$

2. $-\frac{1}{8}h \geq 9$

3. $-\frac{1}{5}y \leq 29$

4. $\frac{1}{3}p < -17$

5. $7g < 42$

6. $36 \geq -9n$

7. $15k < -165$

8. $-8q \leq 64$

9. $9 > -\frac{1}{12}u$

10. $-13c \geq 104$

11. $-\frac{1}{7}b < 61$

12. $-68 \leq -17j$

13. A tuition bill for school states that Brenda owes $438. She wants to pay off her bill in 6 months. Write and solve an inequality that gives the least amount she can repay each month.

14. Mark earns $363 a week. Pedro works for $8.25 an hour. For how many hours must Pedro work to make as much as or more than Mark?

Practice

For use with pages 146–149

Solve the inequality. Then graph its solution.

15. $34 > 4 - 5x$

16. $7y - 12 < 8y + 5$

17. $4p - 21 \geq 7$

18. $3(7 - m) \leq 4(2 - m)$

19. $12d < -5(51 + d)$

20. $13z + 19 \leq 8z - 6$

21. You went to the post office with $20. You mailed a package for $3.67. At most, how many $.37 stamps could you have purchased?

Solve the inequality.

22. $4(x - 12) \geq x + 6$

23. $3(11 - 6x) \geq -3$

24. $9(6 + x) \leq 2(x - 1)$

25. Find the three greatest consecutive integers whose sum is no more than 26.

26. Tickets for a concert were sold for $26 in advance and $31 at the door. Fifty-four tickets were sold in advance. How many tickets need to be sold at the door for an income of at least $5000?

4.1 Practice

For use with pages 168–172

Name _____ Date _____

Write all the factors of the number.

1. 48   **2.** 72   **3.** 93   **4.** 126

Tell whether the number is *prime* or *composite*.

5. 17   **6.** 22   **7.** 74   **8.** 79

Write the prime factorization of the number.

9. 16   **10.** 35   **11.** 50   **12.** 144

Complete the factor tree. Then write the prime factorization of the number.

13.
```
            136
           /    \
       __ ×  4
      / |    |  \
   __ × __ × __ × __
```

14.
```
            90
           /  \
        5  ×  __
             /    \
      __ ×  __ ×  2
     /   \  /  \
  __ ×  __ × __ × __
```

15.

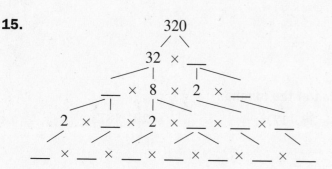

```
                320
               /   \
           32  ×  __
          / |       |  \
       __ × 8 × 2 × __
      / |    |      /  \
   2 × __ × 2 × __ × __ ×
  / \   / \  / \  / \  / \
__ × __ × __ × __ × __ × __ × __
```

LESSON 4.1 Continued

Practice

For use with pages 168–172

Factor the monomial.

16. $8a^2b$ **17.** $30x^2y^2$ **18.** $45m^3n^2$ **19.** $84b^2c^3d$

Write all the factors of the number.

20. 125   **21.** 343   **22.** 693   **23.** 500

24. The eighth-grade class has a total of 162 students. The students need to be divided evenly into homerooms. There needs to be at least 20 students in each homeroom. List all the possible combinations. Which combination makes the most sense? Explain.

25. Write two different factor trees for the number 124. Compare the prime factorization. Are they the same?

Using exponents, write the prime factorization of the number.

26. 360   **27.** 686   **28.** 1728   **29.** 1872

Name _____ Date _____

Practice

For use with pages 173–177

Match the pair of numbers with its GCF.

1. 18, 24   **2.** 16, 36   **3.** 27, 45   **4.** 32, 72

A. 4   **B.** 6   **C.** 8   **D.** 9

Find the greatest common factor of the numbers.

5. 12, 14, 20   **6.** 24, 32, 40   **7.** 21, 42, 56

Decide whether the numbers are relatively prime. If not, find the greatest common factor.

8. 12, 15   **9.** 9, 36   **10.** 26, 39

11. 37, 42   **12.** 27, 70   **13.** 50, 65

14. 64, 80   **15.** 46, 115   **16.** 112, 140

You made muffins for a bake sale. You made 36 blueberry, 52 banana walnut, 48 pumpkin spice, and 24 bran muffins. You want to put an equal number of muffins on each plate. What is the greatest number of plates that you can make?

17. Write the prime factorizations of the numbers 36, 52, 48, and 24.

18. What are the common prime factors of the four numbers?

19. Multiply the common prime factors to get the GCF. What meaning does the GCF have in the problem?

LESSON
4.2 Continued

Name _____ Date _____

Practice

For use with pages 173–177

Find the GCF of the variable expression.

20. $36x^2, 45x^4$
        21. $14xy^2, 28x^2y$
        22. $4x^3y^2, 20xy^3z$

23. $16x^2y, 15y^3z$
        24. $18x^4, 54y^2z$
        25. $52xy^2z, 65x^5yz^2$

26. You are trying to determine the greatest common factor of two numbers. The second number is a multiple of the first number. What will the greatest common factor be? Explain.

27. Cheryl, Mark, Jeremy, and Tonya each work at the same store. Cheryl works 32 hours, Mark works 36 hours, Jeremy works 12 hours, and Tonya works 16 hours a week. The manager of the store wants to make each person work equal length shifts. What is the longest shift that will allow each person's shift to be the same length? How many shifts will each person work?

28. Name two composite numbers that have the greatest common factor 8.

LESSON 4.3

Name _____ Date _____

Practice

For use with pages 179–183

Simplify.

1. $\dfrac{12}{14}$

2. $\dfrac{22}{33}$

3. $\dfrac{34}{36}$

4. $\dfrac{54}{81}$

5. $\dfrac{-26}{65}$

6. $\dfrac{-45}{105}$

7. $\dfrac{13ab}{15a}$

8. $\dfrac{-18xz}{66xyz}$

Tell whether the fractions are equivalent.

9. $\dfrac{5}{9}, \dfrac{30}{54}$

10. $\dfrac{3}{4}, \dfrac{27}{35}$

11. $\dfrac{8}{56}, \dfrac{1}{8}$

12. $\dfrac{7}{17}, \dfrac{28}{68}$

Write two fractions that are equivalent to the given fraction.

13. $\dfrac{64}{84}$

14. $\dfrac{27}{243}$

15. $\dfrac{75}{90}$

16. $\dfrac{120}{132}$

In Exercises 17–20, evaluate the expression when $x = 7$ and $y = 12$.

17. $\dfrac{4x^3}{x^2}$

18. $\dfrac{3y^2}{x^3}$

19. $\dfrac{-8x}{xy}$

20. $\dfrac{9x^5}{12y^3}$

21. Evaluate the expression $\dfrac{13x^4}{-4x}$ when $x = 6$.

Lesson 4.3

Name _____ Date _____

Practice
For use with pages 179–183

Use the information in the table. The table lists the number of items a bakery makes in a day. Write your answer in simplest form.

22. What fraction of the items baked are muffins?

Item	Number Baked
Croissants	64
Muffins	46
Pies	12
Rolls	112

23. What fraction of the items baked are croissants?

24. What fraction of the items baked are rolls?

Write the fractions in simplest form. Tell whether they are equivalent.

25. $\dfrac{24}{28}, \dfrac{48}{56}$

26. $\dfrac{99}{100}, \dfrac{9}{10}$

27. $\dfrac{56}{102}, \dfrac{84}{153}$

28. $\dfrac{84}{91}, \dfrac{154}{169}$

29. $\dfrac{64}{68}, \dfrac{144}{153}$

30. $\dfrac{26}{31}, \dfrac{208}{248}$

Name _____ Date _____

Practice
For use with pages 186–189

Match the pair of numbers with its LCM.

1. 9, 15

2. 21, 14

3. 16, 18

4. 17, 11

A. 144

B. 45

C. 187

D. 42

List the first few multiples of each number. Then use the lists to find the LCM of the numbers.

5. 5, 6

6. 16, 24

7. 15, 45

8. 14, 20

Write the prime factorization of the numbers. Then find their LCM.

9. 12, 72

10. 28, 42

11. 36, 39

12. 20, 70

13. 6, 9, 12

14. 20, 24, 28

15. 14, 21, 30

16. 40, 60, 24

17. 48, 56, 64

Find the LCM of the monomials.

18. $4a^2b, 9ab^2$

19. $5c^3d, 25c^4d^3$

20. $28p^2q^4, 42p^3q$

LESSON 4.4 Continued

Practice

For use with pages 186–189

21. Stephanie gets her hair cut every 42 days. Her sister goes to the same hairdresser and gets her hair cut every 48 days. Both sisters just got their hair cut on the same day. In how many days will they both get their hair cut again?

22. The city's baseball team plays at its home field every 6 days. The same city's football team plays at its home field every 14 days. Both teams just played at their home field on Sunday. In how many more days will this happen again? What day of the week will it be?

Find the LCM of the numbers using prime factorization.

23. 134, 335

24. 242, 264

25. 312, 182

26. 26, 91, 117

27. 16, 32, 48, 60

28. 21, 42, 82, 105

Find the LCM of the monomials.

29. $15x^2y^3, 9x^2y$

30. $22a^4b^7, 44a^4b^5$

31. $28p^4q^2, 12pq^4$

32. Michael, Kyle, and Duane are shooting baskets. Michael makes a basket every 4 shots, Kyle makes a basket every 5 shots, and Duane makes a basket every 3 shots. All three just made a basket. What is the least number of shots they have to take until they all make their baskets at the same time?

Lesson 4.4

Name _____ Date _____

Practice

For use with pages 192–195

Find the least common denominator of the fractions.

1. $\dfrac{5}{6}, \dfrac{13}{24}$

2. $\dfrac{17}{18}, \dfrac{7}{9}$

3. $\dfrac{9}{12}, \dfrac{13}{20}$

4. $\dfrac{3}{14}, \dfrac{4}{15}$

Complete the statement with <, >, or =.

5. $\dfrac{8}{9}$ —— $\dfrac{24}{27}$

6. $\dfrac{7}{10}$ —— $\dfrac{9}{14}$

7. $\dfrac{8}{15}$ —— $\dfrac{15}{24}$

8. $\dfrac{11}{21}$ —— $\dfrac{13}{24}$

9. $3\dfrac{5}{6}$ —— $\dfrac{29}{8}$

10. $\dfrac{134}{30}$ —— $4\dfrac{7}{15}$

11. $1\dfrac{3}{8}$ —— $\dfrac{13}{9}$

12. $\dfrac{9}{28}$ —— $\dfrac{11}{56}$

13. $2\dfrac{8}{17}$ —— $\dfrac{25}{11}$

Order the numbers from least to greatest.

14. $\dfrac{1}{4}, \dfrac{5}{8}, \dfrac{1}{12}, \dfrac{9}{16}$

15. $1\dfrac{15}{18}, \dfrac{5}{6}, \dfrac{13}{9}$

16. $\dfrac{81}{24}, 4\dfrac{2}{3}, \dfrac{28}{8}, \dfrac{65}{18}$

17. $\dfrac{11}{13}, \dfrac{5}{2}, \dfrac{7}{3}, \dfrac{11}{12}$

18. $\dfrac{21}{15}, 2\dfrac{4}{5}, \dfrac{27}{20}, 2\dfrac{10}{12}$

19. $\dfrac{19}{9}, 2\dfrac{1}{12}, \dfrac{34}{15}, \dfrac{41}{18}$

Practice

For use with pages 192–195

20. Shawnda needs $2\frac{3}{5}$ hours to make dinner. Jermaine needs $\frac{54}{21}$ hours to finish making his dinner. Who needs more time to finish making their meal?

21. Brendan has finished 23 of his 50 homework problems. Todd has completed 15 of his 27 homework problems. Write the number of finished problems as a fraction of the total number of homework problems for each person. Who has a greater number of homework problems completed?

22. You read three movie reviews for a movie you want to see. One reviewer gave it 7 out of 10 stars. A second reviewer gave it 3 out of 4 stars. A third reviewer gave it 3 out of 5 stars. Which review had the greatest fraction of stars?

Complete the statement with <, >, or = by first comparing each fraction to $\frac{1}{2}$.

23. $\dfrac{21}{56}$ ——— $\dfrac{59}{78}$

24. $\dfrac{67}{134}$ ——— $\dfrac{35}{70}$

25. $\dfrac{103}{200}$ ——— $\dfrac{57}{120}$

Lesson 4.5

LESSON
4.6

Name _____ Date _____

Practice

For use with pages 196–200

Tell whether the product of powers property can be used to simplify the expression.

1. $8^4 \cdot 8^7$ **2.** $2^3 \cdot 3^2$ **3.** $x^2 \cdot y^5$ **4.** $p^4 \cdot p^6$

Multiply or divide. Write your answer as a power.

5. $6^4 \cdot 6^8$ **6.** $12^3 \cdot 12$ **7.** $x^5 \cdot x^7$ **8.** $a^4 \cdot a^4$

9. $\dfrac{w^{11}}{w^6}$ **10.** $\dfrac{13^{10}}{13^3}$ **11.** $\dfrac{9^8}{9^7}$ **12.** $\dfrac{m^8}{m^2}$

13. $b^4 \cdot b^{13}$ **14.** $\dfrac{k^{15}}{k^8}$ **15.** $(-5)^2 \cdot (-5)^7$ **16.** $\dfrac{(-15)^7}{(-15)^3}$

17. Describe and correct the error in the solution.

$$\begin{aligned} 3^2 \cdot 3^5 &= 3^{2 \cdot 5} \\ &= 3^{10} \end{aligned}$$

Lesson 4.6

Name _____ Date _____

4.6 Continued LESSON **Practice**
For use with pages 196–200

Determine the number that correctly completes the statement.

18. $6^4 \cdot 6^? = 6^{11}$ **19.** $3^2 \cdot \underline{\quad}^4 = 3^6$ **20.** $\dfrac{11^9}{11^?} = 11^8$ **21.** $\dfrac{4^?}{4^6} = 4^7$

Simplify the expression. Write your answer as a power.

22. $4p^2 \cdot 4p^6$ **23.** $11f^8 \cdot 11f^3$ **24.** $6^2a^3b^5 \cdot 6^3a^4b^4$

25. $\dfrac{u^4v^5}{u^2v^4}$ **26.** $\dfrac{z^4 \cdot z^3}{z^2}$ **27.** $\dfrac{12^4r^7}{12^3r^3}$

28. $\dfrac{23^2m^{19}}{23m^{13}}$ **29.** $14r^3s^4 \cdot 14^4r^9s^5$ **30.** $\dfrac{10^7x^{14}y^{12}}{10^3x^4y^9}$

31. The volume of a cube is *side length* $\times$ *side length* $\times$ *side length*. Find the volume of a cube with a side length of 2^3. Write your answer as a power.

32. You have a garden that is 4^2 feet wide and 4^3 feet long. You want to weed your garden. You can weed one square foot of your garden in 30 seconds. Find the area of the garden. How long will it take to weed the whole garden?

56   **Middle School Math, Course 3**
Chapter 4   Practice Workbook

4.7

Name _____ Date _____

Practice

For use with pages 201–204

Evaluate the expression.

1. 5^{-4}

2. $(-8)^{-6}$

3. $4^{-12} \cdot 4^7$

4. 15^0

5. $(-3)^{-4}$

6. $11^{17} \cdot 11^{-16}$

7. $537^{12} \cdot 537^{-12}$

8. 7^{-2}

Write the expression using only positive exponents.

9. $g^{-5} \cdot g^8$

10. $y^{12} \cdot y^{-12}$

11. $7p^{-6}$

12. $j^{-5} \cdot j^{-3} \cdot j^{-8}$

13. $b^8 \cdot b^{-6} \cdot b^{-9}$

14. $\dfrac{6x^{-3}}{x^6}$

15. $\dfrac{c^{-11}}{c^3}$

16. $\dfrac{15d^{-8}}{5d^3}$

17. $\dfrac{26z^{-21}}{2z^9}$

18. $\dfrac{7^{-5}w^4}{7^4}$

19. $\dfrac{14^{-3}t^{-4}s^{11}}{14^8}$

20. $a^9 \cdot a^{-4} \cdot b^8 \cdot b^{-15}$

LESSON
(4.7) Practice
Continued
For use with pages 201–204

Find the missing exponent.

21. $\left(5z^8\right)^? = 1$

22. $7w^? = \dfrac{7}{w^6}$

23. $b^? \cdot b^4 = \dfrac{1}{b^9}$

24. $\dfrac{m^?}{m^4} = \dfrac{1}{m^{11}}$

25. $u^{-5} \cdot u^? = \dfrac{1}{u^{18}}$

26. $\dfrac{f^{-7}}{f^?} = \dfrac{1}{f^{14}}$

27. A measure of force is measured in units called *newtons*. This unit can be expressed as kg • m • s^{-2}. Write the unit without negative exponents.

28. The electric potential of a battery is measured in *volts*. This unit can be expressed as kg • m^2 • A^{-1} • s^{-3}. Write the unit without negative exponents.

29. The mass of one atomic unit (or an atom) is 1.66×10^{-27} kilograms. You can convert this mass to attograms by multiplying the kilograms by 1×10^{-21}. Write the mass of one atom in attograms.

30. The distance from Pluto to the sun is 5.87×10^{12} meters. You can convert the units to terameters by multiplying by 1×10^{-12}. Convert the distance to terameters.

Lesson 4.7

LESSON 4.8

Practice

For use with pages 205–208

Write the number in scientific notation.

1. 730,000　　　　**2.** 6,100　　　　**3.** 8,915,000,000

4. 0.0000748　　　　**5.** 0.00093　　　　**6.** 0.000000056

Write the number in standard form.

7. 8.04×10^{-5}　　　　**8.** 5.26×10^{-13}　　　　**9.** 1.39×10^{-2}

10. 4.11×10^{3}　　　　**11.** 7.61×10^{11}　　　　**12.** 7.45×10^{8}

Write the product in scientific notation.

13. $(7 \times 10^{3}) \times (6 \times 10^{5})$　　　　**14.** $(8 \times 10^{3}) \times (2 \times 10^{4})$

15. $(9.4 \times 10^{2}) \times (1.7 \times 10^{6})$　　　　**16.** $(3.6 \times 10^{9}) \times (8.4 \times 10^{7})$

17. In 1999, 2.16×10^{8} motor vehicles were registered in the United States. Write this number in standard form.

18. The mass of Earth is 5,970,000,000,000,000,000,000,000 kilograms. Write this number in scientific notation.

Complete the statement with <, >, or =.

19. 6.9×10^{3} _____ 6.9×10^{4}　　　　**20.** 8.003×10^{-6} _____ 8.003×10^{-7}

21. 4.25×10^{16} _____ 4.25×10^{15}　　　　**22.** 7.6×10^{-8} _____ 0.76×10^{-7}

Lesson 4.8

Name _____ Date _____

Practice

For use with pages 205–208

Write the product or quotient in scientific notation.

23. $(3.8 \times 10^{-4}) \times (9.2 \times 10^{-8})$

24. $(4.6 \times 10^{6}) \times (8.7 \times 10^{-4})$

25. $(7.5 \times 10^{-8}) \times (1.3 \times 10^{9})$

26. $(6.2 \times 10^{-7}) \times (5.5 \times 10^{-51})$

27. $\dfrac{3.042 \times 10^{10}}{7.8 \times 10^{8}}$

28. $\dfrac{1.19 \times 10^{13}}{1.4 \times 10^{7}}$

29. $\dfrac{3.551 \times 10^{8}}{6.7 \times 10^{5}}$

Use the information in the table. The table lists the number of people in attendance for the Super Bowl. Round your answer to the hundredths place.

30. How many times greater was the attendance in 1978 than in 1997?

31. How many times greater was the attendance in 1980 than in 1992?

Year	Attendance
1977	1.0344×10^{5}
1978	7.5583×10^{4}
1980	1.0399×10^{5}
1992	6.3130×10^{4}
1997	7.2301×10^{4}

Lesson 4.8

Name _____ Date _____

Practice

For use with pages 219–223

1. What subtraction problem does the model represent?

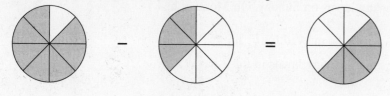

Find the sum or difference.

2. $\dfrac{15}{24} + \dfrac{6}{24}$

3. $\dfrac{4}{9} - \dfrac{7}{9}$

4. $\dfrac{11}{12} - \dfrac{5}{12}$

5. $2\dfrac{3}{4} + \dfrac{3}{4}$

6. $-3\dfrac{4}{5} + 1\dfrac{2}{5}$

7. $\dfrac{8}{21} + \dfrac{6}{21}$

8. $-\dfrac{5}{6} - \left(-\dfrac{1}{6}\right)$

9. $-2\dfrac{1}{4} - 2\dfrac{1}{4}$

10. $4\dfrac{3}{8} + \left(-\dfrac{7}{8}\right)$

In Exercises 11–13, simplify the expression.

11. $\dfrac{5h}{6} + \dfrac{3h}{6}$

12. $\dfrac{3x}{5y} - \dfrac{4x}{5y}$

13. $-\dfrac{5v}{16w} - \dfrac{11v}{16w}$

14. A restaurant serves a steak that weighs $1\dfrac{5}{8}$ pounds. There is a bone in the steak that weighs $\dfrac{7}{8}$ of a pound. How much does the meat weigh?

LESSON 5.1 Continued

Practice

For use with pages 219–223

15. Matthew worked $2\frac{1}{6}$ hours mowing lawns on Sunday. On Monday he mowed for $2\frac{5}{6}$ hours, and on Tuesday he mowed for $1\frac{5}{6}$ hours. What is the total amount of time Matthew spent mowing lawns in the 3 days?

Evaluate.

16. $\frac{9}{14} + \frac{3}{14} + \frac{1}{14}$

17. $-\frac{3}{22} - \frac{7}{22} - \frac{1}{22}$

18. $\frac{5}{9} - 1\frac{7}{9} + \frac{8}{9}$

19. $-\frac{13}{18} + 1\frac{5}{18} - \frac{17}{18}$

20. $-4\frac{9}{20} - 2\frac{13}{20} + \frac{7}{20}$

21. $3\frac{7}{12} - \left(1\frac{5}{12} - \frac{9}{12}\right)$

Solve the equation.

22. $x + \frac{1}{6} = \frac{5}{6}$

23. $\frac{13}{15} - w = \frac{7}{15}$

24. $b - \frac{3}{8} = \frac{7}{8}$

Lesson 5.1

LESSON 5.2

Name ______________________________ Date __________

Practice

For use with pages 224-227

Find the sum or the difference.

1. $\frac{7}{8} - \frac{1}{4}$

2. $\frac{5}{9} + \frac{3}{10}$

3. $\frac{10}{13} + \frac{12}{15}$

4. $-\frac{8}{11} + \frac{3}{8}$

5. $\frac{9}{14} + \frac{-13}{20}$

6. $5\frac{3}{5} - 7$

7. $4\frac{2}{7} - \frac{1}{6}$

8. $2\frac{1}{3} + 6\frac{19}{21}$

9. $\frac{12}{13} + 3\frac{7}{8}$

In Exercises 10–14, use the table that shows the results of a pie eating contest.

10. How many pies did Jim eat?

11. How many pies did Stephanie eat?

12. How many pies did Jamal eat?

13. Who won the pie eating contest?

14. If the people running the contest made 40 pies, how many pies did they have left over after the 3 contestants ate their pies?

	Pies Eaten		
	Apple	**Blueberry**	**Cherry**
Jim	$3\frac{3}{4}$	$2\frac{1}{8}$	$5\frac{2}{5}$
Jamal	$4\frac{3}{8}$	$3\frac{1}{2}$	$3\frac{2}{3}$
Stephanie	$2\frac{3}{5}$	$3\frac{5}{8}$	$5\frac{2}{3}$

Lesson 5.2

Tell whether the statement is *true* or *false*.

15. $\frac{1}{5} + \frac{7}{10} - \frac{3}{20} = \frac{17}{20}$

16. $\frac{16}{27} - \frac{1}{3} + \frac{5}{54} = \frac{19}{54}$

17. $\frac{3}{15} - \frac{7}{12} + \frac{-7}{30} = \frac{-13}{30}$

Name _____ Date _____

Practice

For use with pages 224–227

Simplify the variable expression.

18. $\dfrac{8x}{15} - \dfrac{8x}{9}$

19. $\dfrac{4m}{5} - \dfrac{9m}{11}$

20. $\dfrac{10}{13p} + \dfrac{2}{7}$

21. $\dfrac{17}{24q} + \dfrac{16}{21q}$

In Exercises 22–24, solve the equation.

22. $4\dfrac{7}{8} + 1\dfrac{3}{5} - x = 3\dfrac{39}{40}$

23. $8\dfrac{3}{4} - 2\dfrac{1}{9} - y = 2\dfrac{29}{36}$

24. $w + 3\dfrac{5}{8} - 5\dfrac{1}{4} = 1\dfrac{3}{16}$

25. You need to dig a ditch $15\dfrac{1}{2}$ yards long. You dig $7\dfrac{3}{8}$ yards in the morning and another $3\dfrac{1}{4}$ yards after lunch. How much more of the ditch is left to dig?

LESSON 5.3 Practice

For use with pages 228–233

Find the product.

1. $\dfrac{3}{10} \cdot \dfrac{1}{6}$

2. $\dfrac{7}{21} \cdot \dfrac{8}{9}$

3. $\dfrac{21}{25} \cdot \dfrac{15}{28}$

4. $-9 \cdot \dfrac{1}{9}$

5. $16 \cdot \dfrac{3}{4}$

6. $-18 \cdot \left(-\dfrac{7}{12}\right)$

7. $6\dfrac{4}{9} \cdot 4\dfrac{7}{10}$

8. $-7\dfrac{3}{5} \cdot 3\dfrac{4}{7}$

9. $-12 \cdot \left(-2\dfrac{7}{15}\right)$

Evaluate the expression when $x = \dfrac{7}{10}$ and $y = -\dfrac{11}{12}$.

10. $\dfrac{5}{9}x$

11. $-\dfrac{9}{13}y$

12. xy

13. $-2\dfrac{5}{8}y$

In Exercises 14 and 15, use the following information. Ice hockey is played on a rink that is 61 meters long and $25\dfrac{1}{2}$ meters wide. There are two goals on the hockey rink. Each goal opening has the shape of a rectangle that is $1\dfrac{1}{5}$ meters high and $1\dfrac{4}{5}$ meters wide.

14. What is the area of the ice hockey rink?

15. What is the area of a goal opening?

Lesson 5.3

Practice

For use with pages 228–233

Find the area of the figure.

16.

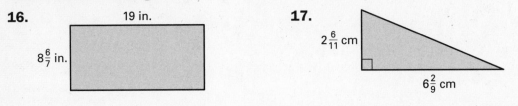

19 in.

$8\frac{6}{7}$ in.

17.

$2\frac{6}{11}$ cm

$6\frac{2}{9}$ cm

In Exercises 18–20, find the product.

18. $\frac{1}{3} \cdot \frac{2}{5} \cdot \left(-\frac{7}{9}\right)$

19. $-\frac{6}{7} \cdot 1\frac{2}{3} \cdot 4\frac{1}{5}$

20. $-7\frac{3}{5} \cdot \left(-1\frac{4}{7}\right) \cdot \frac{5}{8}$

21. Evaluate the expression $\frac{1}{9} + \frac{2}{5} \cdot \frac{11}{15}$.

Lesson 5.3

Name _____ Date _____

Practice

For use with pages 234–239

Write the reciprocal of the number.

1. $\dfrac{3}{17}$
2. $-\dfrac{7}{22}$
3. 12
4. $3\dfrac{9}{10}$

Find the quotient.

5. $\dfrac{1}{4} \div \dfrac{7}{8}$
6. $-\dfrac{2}{9} \div \dfrac{5}{6}$
7. $\dfrac{7}{15} \div \dfrac{11}{14}$

8. $\dfrac{17}{24} \div \left(-\dfrac{8}{13}\right)$
9. $\dfrac{15}{26} \div 5$
10. $\dfrac{18}{33} \div (-12)$

11. $4\dfrac{1}{8} \div 2\dfrac{2}{5}$
12. $7\dfrac{5}{6} \div \left(-9\dfrac{4}{7}\right)$
13. $-6\dfrac{13}{32} \div \left(-3\dfrac{3}{16}\right)$

14. $2\dfrac{17}{20} \div (-4)$
15. $3\dfrac{9}{14} \div 7$
16. $-9\dfrac{4}{21} \div 1\dfrac{8}{9}$

In Exercises 17–19, solve the equation.

17. $\dfrac{7}{8}a = 14$
18. $-\dfrac{9}{10}b = 27$
19. $-14 = -\dfrac{2}{13}w$

Name _____ Date _____

Practice

For use with pages 234–239

20. You mix a quart of grape juice in a pitcher. You are filling juice glasses that each hold $\frac{2}{3}$ cup of juice. There are 4 cups in a quart. How many juice glasses can you fill?

21. A child is playing with blocks and wants to build a house with a roof. The pieces to build the roof are $\frac{3}{4}$ inch wide. The entire roof will be $7\frac{5}{8}$ inches wide. How many pieces laid side-by-side will cover the width?

In Exercises 22–24, evaluate the expression when $x = 3$ and $y = 7$.

22. $\frac{x}{4} \div \frac{9}{120}$

23. $\frac{2}{9}x \div \frac{4y}{15}$

24. $-\frac{20}{y} \div \frac{x}{21}$

25. A team is playing soccer on a field that is $110\frac{2}{5}$ yards long. The field has an area of $10,852\frac{8}{25}$ square yards. How wide is the field?

Lesson 5.4

Name _____ Date _____

Practice

For use with pages 242–246

The diagram shows relationships between types of numbers. Tell which labeled area represents the given number type.

1. Whole numbers

2. Rational numbers

3. Integers

Tell whether the number is included in each of the following number groups: *rational number*, *integer*, *whole number*.

4. 16   **5.** 0.172   **6.** $0.\overline{27}$ **7.** -8

Write the fraction or mixed number as a decimal.

8. $\dfrac{3}{5}$ **9.** $-\dfrac{4}{9}$ **10.** $-\dfrac{9}{11}$ **11.** $\dfrac{11}{16}$

12. $3\dfrac{1}{8}$ **13.** $-5\dfrac{4}{27}$ **14.** $7\dfrac{16}{33}$ **15.** $\dfrac{33}{40}$

16. $-\dfrac{7}{100}$ **17.** $\dfrac{17}{34}$ **18.** $-8\dfrac{19}{50}$ **19.** $-\dfrac{70}{101}$

Write the decimal as a fraction or mixed number.

20. 0.24   **21.** -0.61 **22.** 2.48   **23.** 7.15

24. $-0.\overline{3}$ **25.** 0.95   **26.** $-0.\overline{124}$ **27.** -0.109

Practice

For use with pages 242–246

Order the numbers from least to greatest.

28. $\frac{6}{7}$, 0.8, $\frac{3}{4}$, $\frac{11}{13}$, 0.81

29. $6\frac{1}{5}$, 6.15, 6.3, $6\frac{1}{8}$, $6\frac{2}{19}$

In Exercises 30 and 31, use the table that shows the fraction of attempted passes that were completed by each quarterback one Sunday.

Warner	Collins	Griese	Garcia	Favre
$\frac{26}{39}$	$\frac{22}{26}$	$\frac{14}{20}$	$\frac{27}{36}$	$\frac{29}{44}$

30. Write each fraction as a decimal.

31. Write the names of the quarterbacks in order from the highest to lowest fractions of completed passes.

Name _____ Date _____

Practice

For use with pages 247–250

Find the sum or difference.

1. $6.41 + 12.893$

2. $0.37 + 1.498$

3. $-7.25 + 3.704$

4. $-0.78 + (-2.8)$

5. $8.2 + (-4.516)$

6. $-22.115 + 2.67$

7. $-9.54 - 0.068$

8. $37.24 - (-6.518)$

9. $24.669 - 8.1$

10. $1.45 - 7.3$

11. $25.26 - (-11.047)$

12. $-0.935 - 0.14$

Solve the equation.

13. $f + 5.3 = 36$

14. $-2.64 + g = 5.17$

15. $h - 9.21 = 13.8$

16. $j + 0.545 = 18.23$

17. $k + (-9.32) = -10.764$

18. $-8.54 + m = -23.612$

In Exercises 19–22, use front-end estimation to estimate the sum.

19. $7.612 + 5.93 + 2.87 + 14.11$

20. $20.94 + 12.06 + 13.88 + 17.354$

21. $34.25 + 18.34 + 2.994 + 42.068$

22. $42.87 + 31.652 + 11.0258 + 46.35$

23. This month, Sara had a phone bill that was \$43.15, a cable bill that was \$35.87, and an electric bill that was \$56.23. What was the total of the 3 bills?

Name _____ Date _____

Practice

For use with pages 247–250

In Exercises 24–26, find the perimeter of the figure.

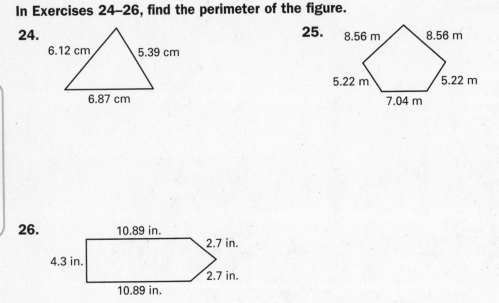

24.
6.12 cm   5.39 cm

6.87 cm

25.
8.56 m   8.56 m

5.22 m   5.22 m

7.04 m

26.
10.89 in.

4.3 in.   2.7 in.

2.7 in.

10.89 in.

27. The number 18.34 can be written as the sum $10 + 8 + 0.3 + 0.04$. Write 175.9231 as a sum in this form.

In Exercises 28–30, use the following information. You need 4.625 yards of fabric to make a dress. You also want to make a matching jacket that requires 2.5 yards of the same fabric.

28. How many yards of fabric will you need to make both pieces?

29. If the store only had one bolt with 7.05 yards of fabric on the bolt, is there enough fabric for you to purchase?

30. What is the difference between what you need and what the store has available?

Lesson 5.6

Name _____ Date _____

Practice
For use with pages 251–254

In Exercises 1–3, place the labels of the steps for dividing decimals in order.

1. _____

2. _____

3. _____

A. Place the decimal point in the quotient so that it lines up with the decimal point in the dividend.

B. Divide.

C. Multiply both the divisor and the dividend by the power of ten that will make the divisor a whole number.

Find the product or the quotient.

4. 8×0.32

5. 7.4×9.1

6. $2.56 \times (-0.7)$

7. $7.2 \div 0.8$

8. $3.675 \div 0.15$

9. $11.26 \div (-0.4)$

10. $24.38 \times (-7.11)$

11. $-26.7804 \div (-6.92)$

12. $115.425 \div 8.1$

13. $12.104 \div 13.6$

14. 0.00075×15.2

15. $54.76 \div 7.4$

In Exercises 16–18, use the following information. The Taj Mahal is a building in Agra, India, that was built by an emperor in memory of his wife. Around the building are rectangular gardens that are 0.305 kilometer wide and 0.305 kilometer long. What is the area of the gardens around the Taj Mahal?

16. Write a verbal model to describe the problem.

17. Substitute the given values and solve.

18. Check to see that your answer is reasonable.

Name _____ Date _____

Practice

For use with pages 251–254

In Exercises 19–24, solve the equation.

19. $-19.95 = -3.2x$ **20.** $8.1w = 7.29$ **21.** $\dfrac{m}{2.41} = 6.6$

22. $\dfrac{g}{-0.0054} = 12.9$ **23.** $0.037y = -0.94128$ **24.** $\dfrac{z}{22.14} = 1.07$

25. You have 5.375 pounds of hamburger for a cookout. You want to make quarter-pound (0.25 pound) hamburger patties. How many patties are you able to make with the meat that you have?

26. You have a photograph that measures 3.5 inches by 6.5 inches. What is the area of the photograph?

In Exercises 27–29, evaluate the expression.

27. $1.3^2 + 3.4 - 6.4 \div 0.8$ **28.** $1.69 \div (1.8 - 0.5) + 2.7$ **29.** $5.25 - 4.73 + 6.1^2$

30. You want to mail a first class letter. The cost is $.37 for the first ounce and $.23 for every ounce after that. How much will it cost to mail a letter that weighs 15 ounces?

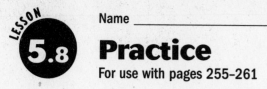

Practice

For use with pages 255–261

In Exercises 1–6, find the mean, median, mode(s), and range of the data.

1. $-21, -6, -15, -49, -52, -6, -26$

2. 104, 98, 73, 16, 29, 83, 66

3. Bowling scores: 114, 136, 220, 245, 179, 150

4. Numbers of cars over a bridge in an hour: 24, 74, 83, 51, 43, 92, 76, 77

5. Numbers of people per family: 7, 4, 3, 2, 6, 4, 5, 2, 3, 4

6. Wages per hour: $7.25, $8.50, $6.50, $7.75, $10

Name _____ Date _____

Practice

For use with pages 255–261

7. The numbers of stories of some tall buildings in Detroit, Michigan, are listed in the table. Find the mean, median, and mode(s) of the number of stories. (Round your answers to the nearest tenth.)

Building	Number of Stories
One Detroit Center	50
Buhl Building	26
Fisher Building	28
Ford Building	19
David Stott Building	37
David Broderick Tower	34

8. The table shows the number of yards several wide receivers gained during their first two football games. Find the mean, median, mode(s), and range of the number of yards gained. Which average do you think best represents the number of yards gained by these receivers over the two games? Explain. (Round your answers to the nearest hundredth.)

Wide Receiver	Number of Yards
Price	265
Mason	227
Moulds	198
Morgan	193
Smith	187
Ward	182
Harrison	178

9. Brian recorded the amount of money he spent over the last 5 days. He knows that the average amount of money he spent was $25.72. On four of the five days, Brian spent $15.50, $28.41, $31.02, and $10.66. Determine how much Brian spent on the fifth day.

10. Find the mean of $5x$, $2x$, $7x$, $-2x$, $-4x$, $7x$, and $-x$.

Name _____ Date _____

Practice

For use with pages 271–275

Decide whether the given value is a solution of the equation. If not, find the solution.

1. $4w - 9(6 - 5w) = 44; w = 3$

2. $9m - 7m - 5 = 17; m = 11$

3. $9x - 8 - 5x = 12; x = 5$

4. $\dfrac{3g - 7}{4} = 8; g = 12;$

Solve the equation. Then check your solution.

5. $6x - 2x - 9 = 7$

6. $15f - 8f + 13 = 55$

7. $2w + 4(7 + 3w) = -14$

8. $4a + 5 - 3a = 27$

9. $-5(w - 3) = 45$

10. $-8m - 9(5 - 3m) = 12$

11. $\dfrac{k - 4}{9} = 3$

12. $\dfrac{3t + 5}{8} = -5$

13. $\dfrac{8c - 4}{7} = 12$

14. Six friends went out to dinner. Each person ordered the same dinner, which cost $15.85. The friends left a combined tip of $14. What was the total of the bill and tip?

Practice

For use with pages 271–275

Lesson 6.1

15. On Friday, you raked leaves for 4 neighbors, on Saturday you raked leaves for 5 neighbors, and on Sunday you raked leaves for 3 neighbors. For these three days, you earned $135. How much money did you earn for each house at which you raked leaves?

Solve the equation. Then check your solution.

16. $7w - 3w + 4w = -15$

17. $6m - 7 - 4m - 16 = -23$

18. $9p + 4(2 + p) = -18$

19. $-19 = \dfrac{28 - k}{16}$

Write an equation for the area of the triangle. Then solve for x.

20. The lengths are in meters.
The area is 348 square meters.

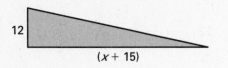

12

$(x + 15)$

21. The lengths are in yards.
The area is 595 square yards.

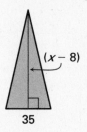

$(x - 8)$

35

Name _____ Date _____

Practice

For use with pages 276–281

Solve the equation. Then check your solution.

1. $8x = 5x + 24$ **2.** $4p = 6p - 12$ **3.** $36 - 2m = 7m$

4. $63 + 11w = 4w$ **5.** $15y - 138 = -8y$ **6.** $-18f = -9f + 72$

7. $17z + 34 = 6z + 56$ **8.** $7g - 15 = -3g + 175$ **9.** $9h + 23 = -7h - 89$

Find the perimeter of the triangle or rectangle. The sides of each triangle are equal in length.

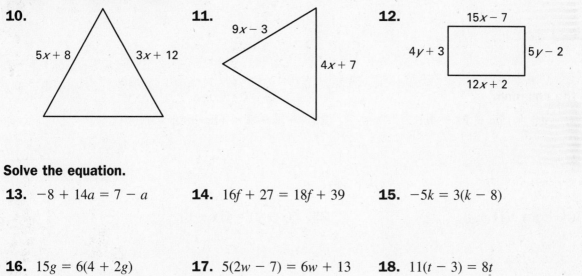

10. $5x + 8$ $3x + 12$

11. $9x - 3$ $4x + 7$

12. $15x - 7$ $4y + 3$ $5y - 2$ $12x + 2$

Solve the equation.

13. $-8 + 14a = 7 - a$ **14.** $16f + 27 = 18f + 39$ **15.** $-5k = 3(k - 8)$

16. $15g = 6(4 + 2g)$ **17.** $5(2w - 7) = 6w + 13$ **18.** $11(t - 3) = 8t$

19. Malcolm planted two trees in his yard. One tree is 50 inches tall and grows at a rate of 2 inches per month. The other tree is 59 inches tall and grows at a rate of 1 inch per month. How many months will it take until both trees are the same height?

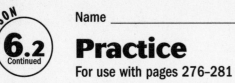

LESSON
6.2
Continued

Name _____ Date _____

Practice
For use with pages 276–281

20. Li Wei and Colleen have the same reading assignment. After one week Li Wei has read 90 pages and Colleen has read 126 pages. If Li Wei can read 30 pages an hour and Colleen can read 24 pages an hour, when will they be on the same page?

21. Roses cost $15 for a dozen, or more if bought individually. You want to purchase 9 dozen and 6 individual roses for centerpiece decorations for a party. For the price of 9 dozen and 6 individual roses you can also purchase 51 individual roses. How much is one rose? How much money do you have to spend on the centerpieces?

Solve the equation.

22. $5m + 18 = 15m - 24 - 4m$

23. $-7q + 2 = 11q - 8q$

24. $3(j + 5) = 5(11 - j)$

25. $6(x + 4) = 2(x + 8)$

26. $5(y - 3) = 8(y + 6)$

27. $8(j - 3) = 4j + 9j - 14$

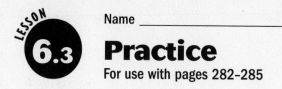

Name _____ Date _____

Practice

For use with pages 282–285

Tell what number you would multiply each side of the equation by to eliminate the decimals or fractions. Then solve the equation.

1. $4.3m - 3.36 = 5.7m$

2. $7.32a = 13.53 + 2.81a$

3. $8.5 - 2.7k = 3.9k - 18.89$

4. $\dfrac{5}{9}w + \dfrac{8}{9} = 3w$

5. $-\dfrac{7}{20}f + \dfrac{2}{5} = \dfrac{1}{4}f$

6. $-\dfrac{1}{7}g + \dfrac{5}{6}g = 9$

7. Describe and correct the error in the solution.

$$\dfrac{7}{9}x + \dfrac{2}{3} = \dfrac{1}{9}x$$

$$\dfrac{2}{3} = -\dfrac{6}{9}x$$

$$2 = -18x$$

$$-\dfrac{1}{9} = x$$

Name _____ Date _____

Practice

For use with pages 282–285

Solve the equation. Check your solution.

8. $m + 6.74 + 0.7m = -3.8$

9. $3.4w - 2.6 - w = 16.6$

10. $9.36k - 2.021 = 8.89k$

11. $g - \dfrac{2}{3}g = -\dfrac{5}{6}$

12. $\dfrac{1}{4}a - \dfrac{4}{9} = \dfrac{7}{9} - \dfrac{5}{6}a$

13. $\dfrac{5}{8}t + \dfrac{2}{15}t = \dfrac{17}{20}$

14. Lisa spends the same amount of time doing homework each day. On Monday, she spent $\dfrac{1}{2}$ of her time studying for a history test. On Tuesday, she spent $\dfrac{3}{5}$ of her time studying for the same test. In the two days, she spent a total of 3 hours and 29 minutes studying for the test. How much time does she spend doing homework each day?

15. Vanessa purchases a pair of jeans for $24.75 and 6 pairs of socks. Jessica buys 2 shirts for $15.60 each and 3 pairs of socks. Both girls spend the same amount and each pair of socks costs the same amount. How much is a pair of socks? How much did each girl spend?

Solve the equation. Check your solution.

16. $4.38c - 3.9 = 14.544 + 1.2c$

17. $0.44(83 - 55b) = -7.04$

18. $\dfrac{5}{9} + \dfrac{5}{12}d = \dfrac{11}{12} + \dfrac{7}{9}d$

19. $7\dfrac{4}{5}f - \dfrac{5}{6} = \dfrac{7}{30}f$

Lesson 6.3

Name _____ Date _____

Practice

For use with pages 288–294

Find the indicated measurement, where _r_ = radius, _d_ = diameter, and _C_ = circumference. Use 3.14 or $\frac{22}{7}$ for π. Explain your choice.

1. $d = 27$ m, $r =$ ____

2. $r = 14$ yd, $d =$ ____

3. $r = 5\frac{1}{6}$ in., $C \approx$ ____

4. $d = 11$ mm, $C \approx$ ____

5. $C = 9.42$ ft, $r \approx$ ____

6. $C = 440$ cm, $d \approx$ ____

Use a ruler to find the indicated measure. Then use the measure to find the circumference of the circle. Use 3.14 for π.

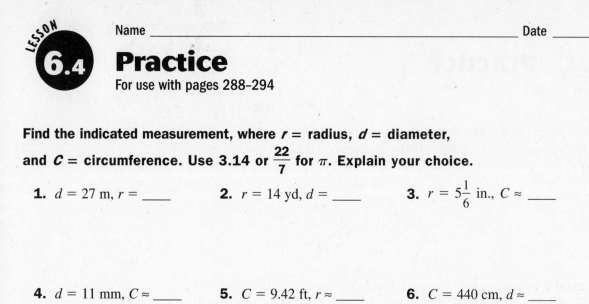

7. $d =$ ____ cm

8. $d =$ ____ mm

9. $r =$ ____ in.

In Exercises 10–12, find the indicated measurement, where _r_ = radius, _d_ = diameter, and _C_ = circumference. Use 3.14 or $\frac{22}{7}$ for π. Explain your choice of value of π.

10. $C = 14.758$ cm

11. $C = 11.932$ cm

12. $C \approx$ ____

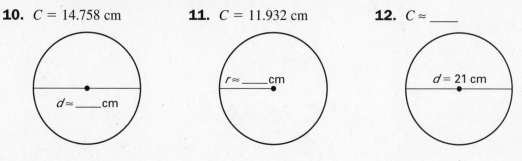

$d \approx$ ____ cm

$r \approx$ ____ cm

$d = 21$ cm

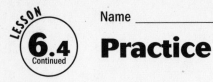
13. The diameter of a dome-shaped camping tent is 9 feet 3 inches. What is the radius of the tent in feet? What is the circumference of the tent in feet? Use 3.14 for π. Round to the nearest hundredth.

14. A circular swimming pool has a circumference of 62 feet 10 inches. What is the diameter of the pool in feet? Use 3.14 for π. Round to the nearest hundredth.

15. The radius of the top of an eraser on a pencil is 3.5 mm. Find the circumference of the eraser.

6.5 **Practice**
For use with pages 295–300

Name _____ Date _____

Solve the inequality. Then graph the solution.

1. $4x + 5 \geq 11$

2. $-2m - 8 \geq -4$

3. $7a + 3 \leq 24$

4. $15 - 9w < -30$

5. $21 + 17y \leq -13$

6. $52 - 28u > 52$

7. $5g - 12 \geq 2g + 18$

8. $9b - 3b + 34 < 2b - 10$

9. $35 - 4f \geq 2f + 7$

10. $4(z - 7) \leq 35$

11. $5(2 - k) > 55$

12. $9(c - 3) < 29 + 2c$

13. As of the 2001 NFL season, the record for the most career yards rushing is 16,726 yards. If a player has 14,925 yards rushing in his career before the start of the 2002 season, what is the least number of yards he needs per game to break the record? Assume there are 16 games in an NFL season. Solve the inequality $16{,}726 \leq 16y + 14{,}925$. Round your answer to the nearest tenth. What does the solution mean in this situation?

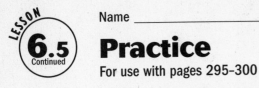

6.5 Continued **Practice**
For use with pages 295–300

14. A ferry boat holds 800 people. There are 260 people already on the boat. The owner of the boat wants to load several tour groups on. The tour groups come in sizes of 40 people or 50 people. The owner would like an equal number of each size of tour group on the boat. What is the greatest number of tour groups that can be loaded onto the boat? Use the verbal model to write an inequality. Then solve the inequality. What does this solution mean in this situation?

Number of people the boat can hold	≥	Number of people already on the boat	+	Number of 40 people tour groups	×	40 people	+	Number of 50 people tour groups	×	50 people

Solve the inequality.

15. $\frac{1}{4}z - 5 \le -\frac{1}{5}z$

16. $\frac{2}{7}h - \frac{1}{3}h > -6$

17. $\frac{4}{11}c - \frac{5}{13}c \le 3$

18. $5.31a - 8.277 \ge 2.64a$

19. $0.4z \ge 9.65 + 0.5z$

20. $5.6p + 2.7p \le 76.36$

21. Frank is trying to save money for college tuition. The college he wants to attend would cost \$13,592 for four years tuition. He has saved \$3,926. He is planning on saving money each month by working for the next three years. At least how much money would he need to save each month so that he has enough to pay for his tuition? Solve the inequality $13{,}592 \le 3{,}926 + 36p$ to find the answer.

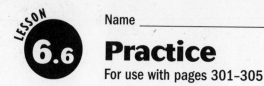

Name _____ Date _____

LESSON 6.6

Practice

For use with pages 301–305

Write the sentence as an inequality. Let *x* represent the unknown number. Then solve the inequality.

1. A number is no more than 12.

2. A number plus 9 is less than 5.

3. Three times a number is at least 20.

4. Eighteen minus a number is at most 19.

In Exercises 5–8, match the verbal expression with the inequality.

A. $7(x + 4) \geq 15$ **B.** $7x + 4 > 15$ **C.** $4x - 7 < 15$ **D.** $4(x - 7) \leq 15$

5. Four times the difference of a number and 7 is no more than 15.

6. Seven times the sum of a number and 4 is at least 15.

7. The sum of seven times a number and 4 is more than 15.

8. The difference of four times a number and 7 is less than 15.

9. You are raising money for a trip. You want to raise at least $500 and have already saved $116. You are going to raise the rest of the money by washing cars. You earn $6 for every car that you wash. Use the verbal model to write and solve an inequality. What is the minimum number of cars that you need to wash in order to obtain this goal?

Money to raise	$\leq$	Number of cars to wash	$\times$	Amount earned per car	$+$	Money already saved

Lesson 6.6

Name _____ Date _____

Practice
For use with pages 301–305

10. Kevin is going to join a swim club. There is a $45 initiation fee. It costs
$28 for each month that he is a member. Kevin only has $300 to pay for
the membership. For how many months can he be a member? Will he be
able to be a member for a full year?

11. A company spent $762,500 to make a movie that will be shown in theaters
for 8 weeks. If the movie makes $1,250,000 in its first week, how much
money does the movie need to earn in the next seven weeks to make a
profit of at least $2,000,000? Write and solve the inequality to determine
this amount.

12. Five friends went out to dinner. Altogether they only had $175 to spend on
the entire meal. They each spent $2 on their beverages and left a tip of $13.
How much can each person spend on his or her own dinner if they each
spend the same amount? Explain how you determined this.

Name _____ Date _____

Practice

For use with pages 317–320

Write the ratio as a fraction in simplest form and two other ways.

1. $\dfrac{32}{40}$

2. $\dfrac{18}{34}$

3. 15 to -35

4. 12 : 8

5. $\dfrac{-6}{20}$

6. 40 : 50

7. 48 to 16

8. $\dfrac{64}{24}$

Write the equivalent rate.

9. $\dfrac{15 \text{ inches}}{1 \text{ second}} = \dfrac{\underline{} \text{ inches}}{1 \text{ minute}}$

10. $\dfrac{12 \text{ minutes}}{1 \text{ quarter}} = \dfrac{\underline{} \text{ seconds}}{1 \text{ quarter}}$

11. $\dfrac{12 \text{ ounces}}{1 \text{ centimeter}} = \dfrac{\underline{} \text{ ounces}}{1 \text{ meter}}$

12. $\dfrac{\$\underline{}}{1 \text{ foot}} = \dfrac{\$6.99}{1 \text{ yard}}$

Write the rate as a unit rate.

13. $\dfrac{216 \text{ points}}{4 \text{ games}}$

14. $\dfrac{800 \text{ people}}{20 \text{ boats}}$

15. $\dfrac{558 \text{ miles}}{9 \text{ hours}}$

16. $\dfrac{144 \text{ hours}}{6 \text{ days}}$

17. $\dfrac{128 \text{ cups}}{4 \text{ gallons}}$

18. $\dfrac{5 \text{ inches}}{8 \text{ years}}$

Name _____ Date _____

Practice

For use with pages 317–320

Find the value of the variable.

19. $\dfrac{x}{7} = \dfrac{3}{21}$

20. $\dfrac{8}{c} = \dfrac{40}{125}$

21. $\dfrac{9}{12} = \dfrac{15}{m}$

22. $\dfrac{6}{15} = \dfrac{f}{35}$

Write the ratio of shaded to unshaded circles.

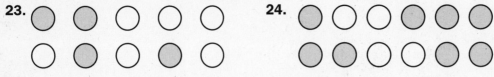

23.

24.

25. Jessica finished a race that was 5 miles long in 30 minutes and 15 seconds. Casey finished a race that was 2 miles long in 11 minutes and 8 seconds. Who has the faster rate? Explain your reasoning.

26. A large can of tomato sauce is 28 ounces and sells for $2.39. A small can of tomato sauce is 6 ounces and sells for $.55. Which can of tomato sauce is the better deal? Explain.

Lesson 7.1

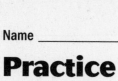

Name _____ Date _____

Practice

For use with pages 321–326

Tell whether the ratios form a proportion.

1. $\frac{7}{9} = \frac{21}{18}$ **2.** $\frac{4}{12} = \frac{5}{15}$ **3.** $\frac{20}{35} = \frac{12}{21}$ **4.** $\frac{52}{70} = \frac{62}{80}$

Solve the proportion.

5. $\frac{4}{7} = \frac{x}{56}$ **6.** $\frac{9}{12} = \frac{21}{m}$ **7.** $\frac{12}{13} = \frac{48}{w}$

8. $\frac{k}{10} = \frac{36}{45}$ **9.** $\frac{21}{42} = \frac{n}{6}$ **10.** $\frac{3.5}{a} = \frac{1.5}{0.3}$

11. $\frac{4.8}{18} = \frac{b}{12}$ **12.** $\frac{56}{1.6} = \frac{35}{f}$ **13.** $\frac{10.8}{c} = \frac{16}{7.6}$

In Exercises 14–19, use the following information. To make a gingerbread house, you use a scale of 1 inch to 12 feet. The house's actual length is given. Find the gingerbread house's length.

14. $\ell = 36$ feet   **15.** $\ell = 108$ feet   **16.** $\ell = 150$ feet

17. $\ell = 210$ feet   **18.** $\ell = 91.2$ feet   **19.** $\ell = 165$ feet

Practice

For use with pages 321–326

20. In one basketball league, there are 96 players on 8 teams. In another basketball league, there are 12 teams. All of the teams in both leagues have the same number of players. How many players are in the 12-team league?

21. A car is able to get 25 miles per gallon of gasoline. The car has a 16 gallon gasoline tank. How many miles can the car travel if you start the trip with a full tank?

Find the value of x.

22. $\dfrac{x + 2}{3} = \dfrac{42}{18}$

23. $\dfrac{x - 3}{8} = \dfrac{28}{32}$

24. $\dfrac{12}{x + 4} = \dfrac{84}{49}$

25. A flower delivery person is able to make 7 deliveries in 30 minutes. He has 3 more hours left to work today. With his remaining time on the job, how many more deliveries can he make?

26. A game show contestant scored 72,500 points during her 5 days on the show. If she earned the same number of points each day, how many points had she earned after being a contestant for only 2 days?

Name _____ Date _____

Practice

For use with pages 327–330

Use a percent proportion. Round to the nearest hundredth if necessary.

1. 72 is what percent of 90?

2. 51 is what percent of 60?

3. 22 is what percent of 121?

4. 40 is what percent of 540?

5. What number is 15% of 80?

6. What number is 84% of 106?

7. What number is 23% of 62?

8. What number is 22% of 35?

9. 32 is 25% of what number?

10. 672 is 80% of what number?

11. 52 is 12.5% of what number?

12. 639 is 36% of what number?

13. On your math test, you scored an 85%. You got 34 problems correct. How many problems were on the test?

14. Steve has $360 in his savings account in the bank. He earns 3% interest each month. How much interest would he earn in 1 month?

Practice

For use with pages 327–330

Use a percent proportion.

15. 436 is what percent of 250?

16. 3.2 is what percent of 25?

17. What number is 156% of 208?

18. What number is 0.3% of 96?

19. 164 is 184% of what number?

20. 72 is 0.04% of what number?

21. A field goal kicker makes 84% of the field goals he attempts. He has attempted 50 field goals this season. How many field goals has he made?

22. Viktor earned $240 this month. He earned $150 of that money mowing lawns. What percent of the money he earned was earned by mowing lawns?

23. There are 450 children that attend a high school. Of those students, 28% are in the marching band. How many students are not in the marching band?

24. The original seating capacity of the University of Michigan stadium was 72,000 people. In 1998, the stadium was expanded to hold another 35,501 people. By what percent did the seating capacity for the new stadium increase?

25. While grocery shopping, you purchase 3 gallons of milk that cost $2.19 a piece. The entire grocery bill came to a total of $52.56. What percent of your grocery bill did you spend on milk?

Write and solve the percent proportion in terms of *y*.

26. What number is 42% of 36*y*?

27. 8*y* is 40% of what number?

Name _____ Date _____

Practice
For use with pages 331–335

Write the decimal or fraction as a percent.

1. 0.05

2. 24.56

3. 0.362

4. 0.007

5. $\frac{3}{8}$

6. $\frac{43}{50}$

7. $\frac{23}{10}$

8. $\frac{50}{80}$

9. 21.4

10. 1.237

11. $\frac{351}{300}$

12. $\frac{275}{500}$

Write the percent as a decimal and as a fraction in simplest form.

13. 40%

14. 35%

15. 18%

16. 104%

17. 56.25%

18. 84.15%

19. 0.2%

20. 138.4%

Order the numbers from least to greatest.

21. $\frac{11}{20}$, 52%, 0.51, 0.055, $\frac{5}{100}$

22. 94%, 0.97, $\frac{14}{15}$, $\frac{27}{30}$, 91%, 0.923

23. 0.037, 3.16%, 0.0328, $\frac{1}{32}$, $\frac{4}{105}$

24. $\frac{7}{9}$, 75%, 0.742, 0.788, $\frac{19}{25}$, $\frac{38}{49}$

Name _____ Date _____

Practice

For use with pages 331–335

The circle graph shows the results of a survey on the colors of homes in a neighborhood. Each fraction in the graph represents part of the total number of homes.

25. Which home color is the most popular?

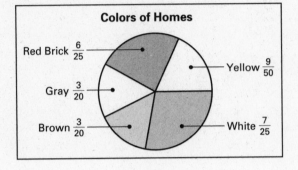

Colors of Homes

Red Brick $\frac{6}{25}$

Gray $\frac{3}{20}$

Brown $\frac{3}{20}$

Yellow $\frac{9}{50}$

White $\frac{7}{25}$

26. What percent of the homes were yellow?

27. What percent of the homes were either white or gray?

28. What percent of the homes were not brown?

Complete the statement using <, >, or =.

29. $\frac{3}{4}$ _____ 78%

30. 126% _____ $\frac{10}{8}$

31. $\frac{14}{16}$ _____ 0.88

32. 7.6% _____ 0.076

33. 67.5% _____ $\frac{135}{200}$

34. 95% _____ 0.975

Lesson 7.4

LESSON 7.5

Practice

For use with pages 338–341

Tell whether the percent change is an *increase* or *decrease*. Then find the percent of change. Round your answer to the nearest tenth.

1. $50,000 to $40,000

2. 5 miles to 12 miles

3. 600 pounds to 550 pounds

4. 2 rabbits to 32 rabbits

5. 120 pages to 200 pages

6. 360 yards to 275 yards

Use the percent of change equation to find the new amount. Round your answer to the nearest tenth.

7. 350 increased by 7%

8. 92 decreased by 4%

9. 845 decreased by 50%

10. 216 increased by 27%

11. 32,250 increased by 42%

12. 92,400 decreased by 82%

In 1860, the population of San Francisco, California, was 56,802. The population increased to 416,912 by 1910, and to 776,773 by 2000. Round your answer to the nearest hundredth.

13. What was the percent increase in the population between 1860 and 1910?

14. What was the percent increase in the population between 1910 and 2000?

15. What was the overall percent increase in population between 1860 and 2000?

LESSON

7.5
Continued

Name _____ Date _____

Practice

For use with pages 338–341

Find the percent of increase or decrease.

16. x to $3x$

17. $2b$ to $5b$

18. w to $\frac{7}{10}w$

19. $2.5a$ to $12.5a$

20. Hugh Duffy holds the highest recorded single-season batting average at 0.440. Over his 10 year career, his batting average was 0.324. What is the percent increase of his best season over his career average?

In Exercises 21–24, use the table that shows the seating capacity of the stadium at the University of Tennessee. Round your answer to the nearest tenth.

21. What was the percent increase in the stadium capacity between 1920 and 1929?

22. What was the percent increase in the stadium capacity between 1938 and 1968?

23. What was the percent increase in the stadium capacity between 1968 and 1980?

24. What was the overall percent increase in the stadium capacity between 1920 and 2000?

Stadium Seating Capacity	
Year	**Capacity**
1920	3,200
1929	17,860
1938	31,390
1968	64,429
1980	91,249
1996	102,544
2000	104,079

Name _____ Date _____

Practice
For use with pages 342–346

Find the sale price or retail price. Round to the nearest cent.

1. Original price: $45
Percent discount: 15%

2. Wholesale price: $17.25
Percent markup: 60%

3. Wholesale price: $130
Percent markup: 100%

4. Original price: $63.50
Percent discount: 25%

5. Original price: $27.99
Percent discount: 30%

6. Wholesale price: $36
Percent markup: 120%

Find the total cost. Round to the nearest cent.

7. Original price: $48.50
Sales tax: 6%

8. Original price: $87
Sales tax: 4.5%

9. Food bill: $45
Tip: 18%
Sales tax (on food only): 5.5%

10. Food bill: $23.80
Tip: 20%
Sales tax (on food only): 6%

11. The wholesale price for a CD is $1.75. A store marks the price of the CD up to $15.99. What is the percent markup for the CD?

12. Shawn got a haircut at the barber shop. It cost $11, and he left a $3 tip. What percent tip did he leave the barber?

Name _____ Date _____

Practice

For use with pages 342–346

13. A store usually sells two rolls of wallpaper for $49.90. The store is running a special, two rolls of wallpaper for $42.42. What is the percent discount?

Tell whether the new price is a *discount* or *markup*. Then find the percent of discount or markup.

14. Old price: $19
New price: $16.15

15. Old price: $39
New price: $44.85

16. Old price: $18
New price: $17.46

17. Old price: $58
New price: $48.72

18. Old price: $160.99
New price: $209.29

19. Old price: $79.50
New price: $143.10

20. You went to a restaurant and spent $53.25 on the meal. There was a 6% sales tax. What was the amount of money, not including a tip, you spent at the restaurant?

21. The wholesale price of a couch is $235. A store marks up the price by 169%. When the couch does not sell, the store offers a 20% discount. What was the original price of the couch? What was the price of the couch after the discount?

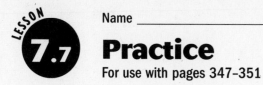

Solve using the percent equation.

1. What number is 68% of 290?

2. What number is 29% of 360?

3. What number is 150% of 8?

4. What number is 0.2% of 980?

5. 117 is 30% of what number?

6. 39.2 is 140% of what number?

7. 56.43 is 19% of what number?

8. 625.6 is 68% of what number?

9. 483.6 is what percent of 180?

10. 69.19 is what percent of 629?

11. 102.08 is what percent of 352?

12. 1.572 is what percent of 524?

Find the amount of simple interest earned.

13. Principal: $620
Annual rate: 3.5%
Time: 2 years

14. Principal: $500
Annual rate: 6.5%
Time: 32 months

15. Principal: $750
Annual rate: 3.5%
Time: 18 months

16. Principal: $2000
Annual rate: 4%
Time: 5 years

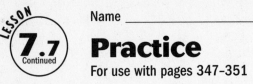

Name _____ Date _____

Practice

For use with pages 347–351

17. How much money must you deposit into a savings account that has a 3% annual interest rate to earn $100 in 3 years?

18. Carl has completed 20% of his 45 credits towards earning his college degree. Write an equation and a proportion that could be used to determine how many credits he has already taken. Then solve both the equation and the proportion. Do you get the same result?

19. A university has an enrollment of 15,057 students. The school has a 65% 4-year graduation rate, and 79% of the students will graduate within 6 years. How many of the students will graduate in 4 years? How many of the students will graduate within 6 years?

Complete the statement with <, >, or =.

20. 92% of 36 _____ 36% of 92

21. 140% of 78 _____ 78% of 140

22. A car manufacturer produces 150,000 sports cars per year. They install either a V-6 or a V-8 engine, and each can be used with an automatic or a manual transmission. Seventy percent of the vehicles have the V-6 engine, and 70% of those V-6s have an automatic transmission. How many cars have a V-6 engine and an automatic transmission? What percentage of the 150,000 cars have the V-6 engine and the automatic transmission?

Lesson 7.7

Name _____ Date _____

Practice

For use with pages 352–357

You randomly draw a card from a bag that contains 3 A-cards, 2 T-cards, 7 B-cards, 5 E-cards, and 8 M-cards. Find the probability of the event.

1. You draw an E.

2. You draw a T.

3. You draw an A or a M.

4. You draw a B or a T.

5. You draw a vowel.

6. You draw an H.

Torry played on a baseball team last year. He had a total of 235 at-bats. The results of his at-bats are shown in the table. Find the experimental probability of the event.

7. He hit a single.

8. He struck out.

Result	Outcome	Result	Outcome
single	32	walk	12
double	23	strike out	41
triple	11	fly out	60
home run	5	ground out	51

9. He hit either a double or a triple.

10. He got a fly out or a ground out.

11. He hit the ball to get on base.

Middle School Math, Course 3 **103**
Chapter 7   Practice Workbook

Name _____ Date _____

Practice

For use with pages 352–357

You randomly draw a marble from a bag of 320 marbles. You record its color and replace it. Use the results shown in the table to estimate the number of marbles in the bag that are the given color.

12. Blue   **13.** Purple

Blue	Green	Purple
10	8	2

14. Green   **15.** Red

16. In a survey of 1240 people, 1054 people said that they had a pet. Also in the survey, 465 people said that they had a cat. What is the probability that a randomly chosen person from this survey has a pet? What is the probability that a randomly chosen person from this survey has a cat?

Find the probability of the event.

17. *Not* rolling a 5 on a number cube

18. *Not* rolling an even number on a number cube

19. *Not* spinning an E on the spinner

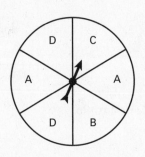

20. Spinning A, B, or D on the spinner

21. You have wrapped 5 presents that are for adults and 4 presents that are for children. You want to give your cousin Sara a gift for a child, but you don't remember which presents are for adults or children. What is the probability that you choose a present at random and it's for a child?

Lesson 7.8

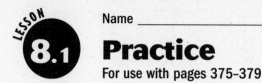

Complete the statement.

1. A straight angle is an angle with a measure of _____.

2. A _____ angle measures 90°.

3. Supplementary angles are two angles whose measures add up to _____.

4. _____ angles are two angles whose measures add up to 90°.

5. _____ angles are a pair of angles, formed by two intersecting lines, that don't share a side.

6. Perpendicular lines are two lines that intersect at a _____ angle.

7. _____ lines are two lines in the same plane that do not intersect.

Tell whether the angles are *complementary, supplementary,* or *neither.*

8. $m\angle 1 = 38°$, $m\angle 2 = 142°$

9. $m\angle 1 = 93°$, $m\angle 2 = 15°$

10. $m\angle 1 = 36°$, $m\angle 2 = 54°$

11. $m\angle 1 = 103°$, $m\angle 2 = 77°$

Find the angle measure.

12. $\angle 1$ and $\angle 2$ are supplementary, and $m\angle 1 = 27°$. Find $m\angle 2$.

13. $\angle 3$ and $\angle 4$ are complementary, and $m\angle 4 = 64°$. Find $m\angle 3$.

In Exercises 14 and 15, find the measures of the numbered angles.

14.

1
2 83°
3

15.

6
5 7
19°

Name _____ Date _____

Practice

For use with pages 375–379

16. In the diagram, $m\angle3 = 123°$. Find the measure of each angle.

Find the value of the variable and the angle measures.

17. $m\angle1 = 3x°$ and $m\angle3 = (7x - 40)°$

18. $m\angle7 = 4x°$ and $m\angle8 = (96 + 3x)°$

19. $m\angle6 = (6 + 2x)°$ and $m\angle5 = (3x - 17)°$

Name _____ Date _____

Practice

For use with pages 382–385

Classify the angle as *acute*, *right*, **or** *obtuse*.

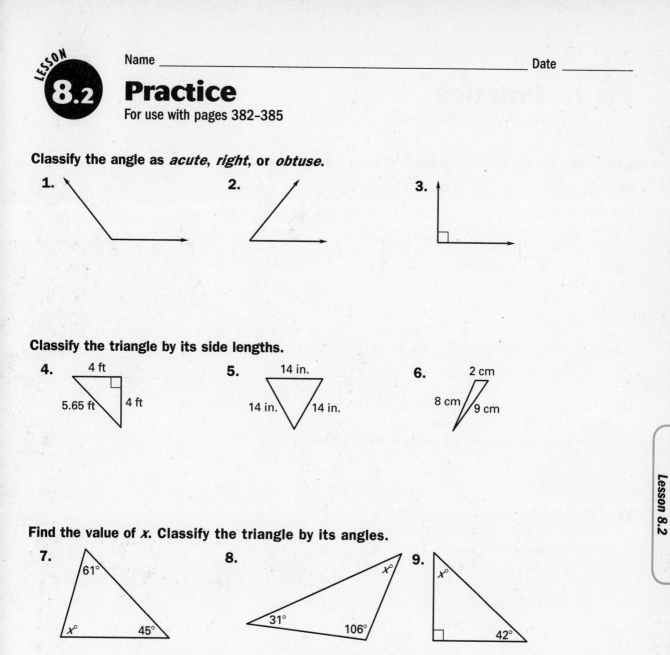

1.

2.

3.

Classify the triangle by its side lengths.

4. 4 ft
5.65 ft   4 ft

5. 14 in.
14 in.   14 in.

6. 2 cm
8 cm   9 cm

Find the value of x. Classify the triangle by its angles.

7. 61° x° 45°

8. 31° x° 106°

9. x° 42°

Can the angles in a triangle have the measures given? Explain.

10. 67°, 108°, 15°

11. 163°, 10.7°, 6.3°

12. $22\frac{2}{3}°$, $57\frac{1}{3}°$, 100°

Lesson 8.2

Name _____ Date _____

Practice
For use with pages 382–385

In Exercises 13–15, find the measure of each angle in the triangle.

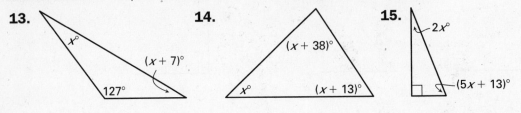

13. $x°$ $(x + 7)°$ $127°$

14. $(x + 38)°$ $x°$ $(x + 13)°$

15. $2x°$ $(5x + 13)°$

16. You are making a quilt that uses triangles. Each of the triangular pieces has sides with lengths of 17 centimeters, 14 centimeters, and 14 centimeters. What kind of triangle are you using to make the quilt?

17. A baseball diamond can be split into two triangles. Classify the triangles formed by their sides and angles.

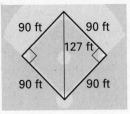

90 ft 90 ft 127 ft 90 ft 90 ft

LESSON 8.3 Practice

For use with pages 386–389

Complete the statement.

1. A quadrilateral is a closed figure with _____ sides that are line segments.

2. A _____ is a quadrilateral with exactly 1 pair of parallel sides.

3. A parallelogram is a quadrilateral with 2 pairs of _____ opposite sides.

4. A _____ is a parallelogram with 4 sides of equal length.

5. A rectangle is a parallelogram with 4 _____ angles.

6. A square is a parallelogram with _____ sides of equal length and _____ right angles.

Classify the quadrilateral.

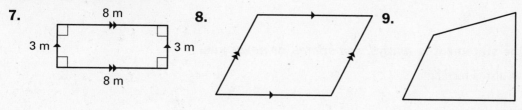

7. 8 m / 3 m / 3 m / 8 m

8.

9.

In Exercises 10–13, find the value of x.

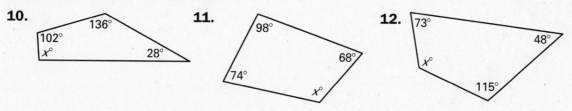

10. 136° / 102° / $x°$ / 28°

11. 98° / 74° / 68° / $x°$

12. 73° / 48° / $x°$ / 115°

13. The angles of a quadrilateral measure 65°, 87°, 106°, and $x°$.

Lesson 8.3

LESSON
8.3
Continued

Name _____ Date _____

Practice

For use with pages 386–389

Find the value of *x* and the unknown angle measures.

14.

$(4x + 8)°$

$(9x - 43)°$

$(8x + 9)°$ $(5x + 48)°$

15.

$(9x + 59)°$ $(6x - 6)°$

$(3x + 8)°$ $(12x + 29)°$

Tell whether the statement is *always*, *sometimes*, or *never* true.

16. A square is also a rectangle.

17. A parallelogram is also a trapezoid.

18. A square is also a rhombus.

19. A quadrilateral is also a parallelogram.

Lesson 8.3

Name _____ Date _____

Practice

For use with pages 390–393

Tell how many sides the given type of polygon has.

1. hexagon

2. heptagon

3. octagon

4. pentagon

5. 12-gon

6. *n*-gon

Tell whether the figure is a *polygon*, a *regular polygon*, or *not a polygon*.

7.

8.

9.

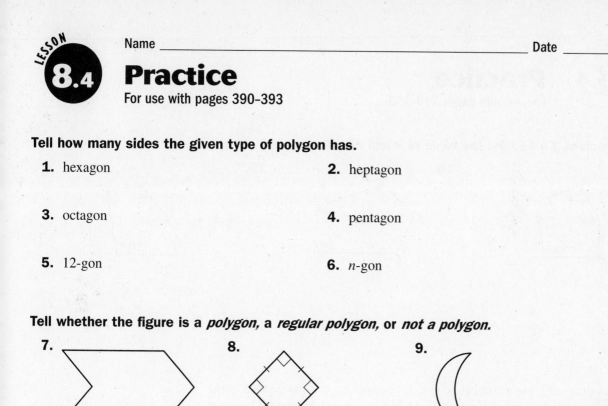

In Exercises 10–12, find the measure of one angle in the polygon.

10. regular 10-gon

11. regular 18-gon

12. regular 24-gon

13. Find the sum of the angle measures in a 14-gon.

Find the value of *x*.

14.

15.

16.

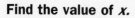
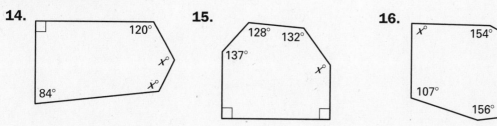

Practice

For use with pages 390–393

In Exercises 17–19, find the value of x and all unknown angle measures.

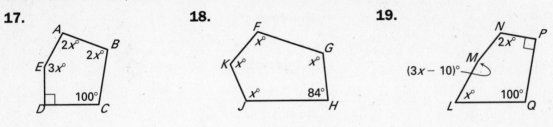

17.

18.

19.

20. A dragonfly has a compound eye. Its compound eye can contain up to 50,000 hexagonal-shaped facets. Sketch a picture of a regular hexagon. What is the measure of one angle of the regular hexagon?

Lesson 8.4

Name _____ Date _____

Practice

For use with pages 396–401

In Exercises 1–5, use the diagram and the fact that quadrilateral *JKLM* ≅ quadrilateral *WXYZ*.

1. Name four pairs of congruent angles.

2. Name four pairs of congruent sides.

3. Find $m\angle K$, $m\angle W$, and $m\angle Z$.

4. Find the length of $\overline{JK}$.

5. Find the length of $\overline{YZ}$.

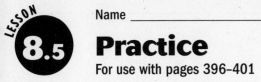

6. Name all the congruent triangles shown.

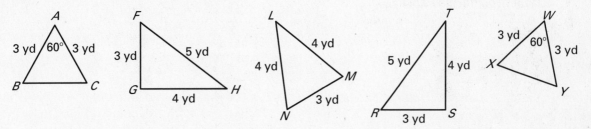

Explain how you know that the two triangles are congruent.

7. $\angle ABC \cong \angle ABD$

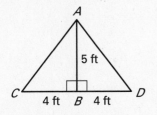

8. $\angle CDE \cong \angle FED$

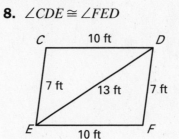

Name _____ Date _____

Practice
For use with pages 396–401

**In Exercises 9–11, explain how you know the triangles are congruent.
Then write an equation and solve for *x*.**

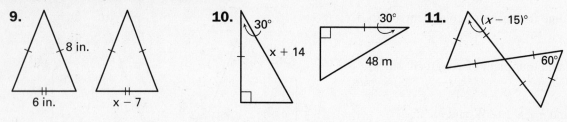

9.

8 in.

6 in.   x − 7

10.   30°

x + 14

30°

48 m

11.   (x − 15)°

60°

12. Stop signs are made in the shape of a regular octagon. Are *any* two regular octagons congruent? Explain.

Name _____ Date _____

Practice

For use with pages 402–408

Tell whether the dashed figure is a reflection of the solid figure.

1.

2.

3.

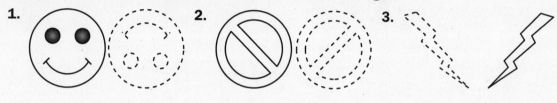

In Exercises 4–6, how many lines of symmetry does the design have?

4.

5.

6.

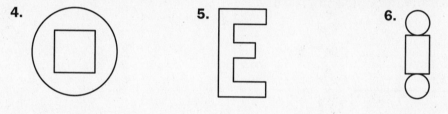

7. The triangle with vertices $A(2, -2)$, $B(2, -5)$, and $C(7, -5)$ is reflected in the x-axis. Find the coordinates of the vertices of the image.

8. The triangle with vertices $X(-3, -1)$, $Y(-4, -5)$, and $Z(2, 3)$ is reflected in the y-axis. Find the coordinates of the vertices of the image.

In Exercises 9–12, reflect the polygon in the given axis. Graph the figure and its image.

9. $A(4, 3)$, $B(1, 7)$, $C(1, 0)$, $D(4, 0)$; x-axis

Practice

For use with pages 402–408

Lesson 8.6

10. $W(-1, 1)$, $X(0, 4)$, $Y(-3, 2)$, $Z(-5, -2)$; y-axis

11. $J(2, -1)$, $K(4, 2)$, $L(7, 1)$, $M(9, -2)$, $N(5, -5)$; y-axis

12. $E(-2, 2)$, $F(2, 2)$, $G(5, 0)$, $H(5, -3)$, $I(0, -2,)$, $J(0, 0)$; x-axis

Give an example of a letter with the given number of lines of symmetry.

13. 1   **14.** 2

How many lines of symmetry does the quilt square have?

15.   **16.**   **17.**

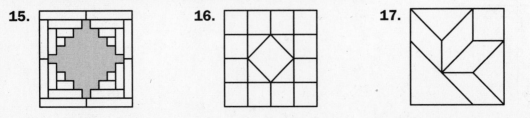

Name _____ Date _____

Practice

For use with pages 409–413

Describe the translation from the solid figure to the dashed figure.

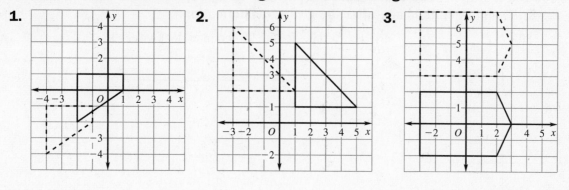

1.   **2.**   **3.**

In Exercises 4–6, name the transformation shown in the graph.

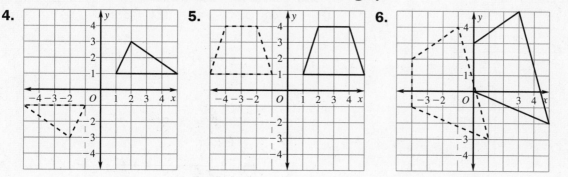

4.   **5.**   **6.**

7. $\triangle XYZ$ has vertices $X(2, 2)$, $Y(-3, 5)$, and $Z(-7, -4)$. Find the vertices of its image after the translation $(x, y) \rightarrow (x - 3, y - 2)$.

8. $\triangle LMN$ has vertices $L(-2, 3)$, $M(2, 6)$, and $N(0, -1)$. Find the vertices of its image after the translation $(x, y) \rightarrow (x - 1, y + 4)$.

Name _____ Date _____

Practice

For use with pages 409–413

**In Exercises 9–14, graph △*ABC* with vertices *A*(–4, –1), *B*(–6, –5),
and *C*(–1, –8). Then graph its image after the given transformation.**

9. Rotate 180°.

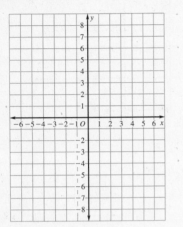

10. Rotate 90° counterclockwise.

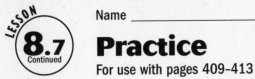

11. Translate using $(x, y) \rightarrow (x + 3, y - 1)$

12. Rotate 180° then translate
using $(x, y) \rightarrow (x + 1, y + 3)$.

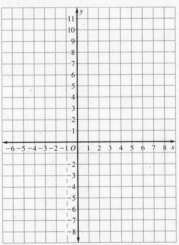

13. Rotate 90° clockwise three times.

14. Translate using $(x, y) \rightarrow (x + 2, y - 4)$
then translate using $(x, y) \rightarrow (x - 3, y - 1)$.

Name _____ Date _____

Practice

For use with pages 416–421

In Exercises 1 and 2, name the similar polygons.

1.

2.

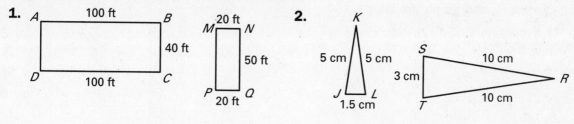

3. △ABC is similar to △RST. Find the value of x.

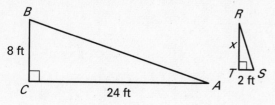

4. Quadrilateral WXYZ is similar to quadrilateral LMNP. Find the values of x and y.

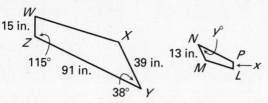

Lesson 8.8

Name _____ Date _____

Practice

For use with pages 416–421

In Exercises 5–9, graph the polygon with the given vertices. Dilate by the scale factor, k, and graph the image.

5. $A(-1, 1)$, $B(2, 1)$, $C(4, 4)$, $D(1, 4)$; $k = 3$

6. $W(1, 6)$, $X(5, 4)$, $Y(4, -1)$; $k = 4$

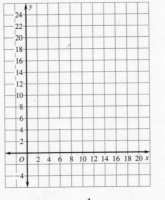

7. $L(0, 0)$, $M(0, -6)$, $N(-6, -9)$, $Q(-3, -3)$; $k = \dfrac{1}{3}$

8. $E(10, 5)$, $F(5, 0)$, $G(5, -5)$, $H(10, -5)$; $k = \dfrac{2}{5}$

9. $J(-2, -2)$, $K(2, 0)$, $L(5, 0)$,
$M(8, -2)$, $N(5, -4)$, $Q(2, -4)$; $k = 2$

10. Brad had planned to put in a rectangular garden that was 12 feet by 8 feet. He decided that it was too big. He decided to reduce the dimensions of the garden by half. How do the areas of the original and revised gardens compare?

Lesson 8.8

Name _____ Date _____

Practice

For use with pages 431–436

Evaluate the square root.

1. $\sqrt{16}$ **2.** $-\sqrt{36}$ **3.** $\sqrt{225}$ **4.** $-\sqrt{400}$

Approximate the square root to the nearest whole number.

5. $\sqrt{15}$ **6.** $\sqrt{48}$ **7.** $\sqrt{79}$ **8.** $\sqrt{140}$

Use a calculator to approximate the square root. Round to the nearest tenth, if necessary.

9. $\sqrt{32}$ **10.** $\sqrt{61.08}$ **11.** $-\sqrt{88.36}$ **12.** $\sqrt{2750}$

13. $\sqrt{3249}$ **14.** $\sqrt{26.94}$ **15.** $\sqrt{4210}$ **16.** $-\sqrt{1089}$

Solve the equation. Check your solutions.

17. $x^2 = 64$ **18.** $q^2 = 100$ **19.** $m^2 - 144 = 0$

20. $w^2 + 97 = 113$ **21.** $f^2 - 64 = 353$ **22.** $a^2 + 31 = 607$

9.1 Practice

Continued

For use with pages 431–436

In Exercises 23–28, solve the equation. Round to the nearest hundredth, if necessary. Check your solutions.

23. $w^2 + 13 = 46$

24. $g^2 - 83 = 19$

25. $55 + p^2 = 173$

26. $a^2 - 76 = 188$

27. $z^2 - 53 = 201$

28. $106 + h^2 = 467$

29. A square ice skating rink has an area of 1849 square feet. What is the perimeter of the rink?

Evaluate the expression $\sqrt{x^2 + y^2}$ for the given values.

30. $x = 9, y = 12$

31. $x = 3, y = 4$

32. $x = 8, y = 6$

Find the two square roots of the number.

33. 0.64

34. 0.09

35. 1.69

36. 5.29

Find the square root.

37. $\sqrt{\dfrac{1}{9}}$

38. $\sqrt{\dfrac{25}{36}}$

39. $\sqrt{\dfrac{49}{81}}$

40. $\sqrt{\dfrac{100}{121}}$

Name _____ Date _____

Practice

For use with pages 437–441

Tell whether the number is *rational* or *irrational*. Explain your reasoning.

1. $\sqrt{360}$

2. $\frac{2}{11}$

3. $\frac{3}{10}$

4. $\sqrt{15}$

5. $\sqrt{\frac{7}{19}}$

6. $\sqrt{8100}$

7. $\frac{5}{16}$

8. $\sqrt{\frac{196}{225}}$

Graph the pair of numbers on a number line. Then complete the statement with <, >, or =.

9. $\frac{3}{8}$ ____ $\sqrt{\frac{3}{8}}$

10. $\frac{7}{11}$ ____ $\sqrt{\frac{49}{121}}$

11. $\sqrt{18}$ ____ 4.8

Order the decimals from least to greatest.

12. $0.31, 0.3\overline{1}, 0.3\overline{13}, 0.3\overline{11}, 0.3\overline{1}$

13. $-0.9\overline{4}, -0.949, -0.9\overline{4}, -0.9\overline{44}$

Evaluate the expression when $a = 4$, $b = 8$, and $c = 12$. Round to the nearest hundredth, if necessary. Tell whether the original result is *rational* or *irrational*.

14. $\sqrt{a + b}$

15. $\sqrt{b^2}$

16. $\sqrt{c + a}$

17. $\sqrt{c - a}$

Lesson 9.2

Order the numbers from least to greatest.

18. $7.4, \sqrt{53}, -8, -8.15$

19. $\sqrt{64}, 8.2, \sqrt{137}, -3$

20. $-\sqrt{21}, -\sqrt{\dfrac{2}{5}}, -4.7, -\dfrac{5}{9}$

21. $3.64, \sqrt{4.8}, \sqrt{8.61}, \dfrac{12}{5}$

22. You are tiling a room in your home that measures 18 feet long by 12 feet wide. Each square tile has an area of 324 square inches. What are the dimensions of a tile? How many tiles will you need to cover the floor?

23. The area of a circle is found by the equation $A = \pi \cdot r^2$, where A is the area and r is the radius. If you know the area, you can calculate the radius of the circle from the equation $r = \sqrt{\dfrac{A}{r}}$. Find the radius of a circle that has an area of 38.6 square centimeters. Round your answer to the nearest hundredth. Use 3.14 for π.

Name _____ Date _____

Practice

For use with pages 442–447

Let *a* and *b* represent the lengths of the legs of a right triangle, and let
c represent the length of the hypotenuse. Find the unknown length.

1. $a = 6$, $b = 8$, $c =$ _____

2. $a =$ _____, $b = 24$, $c = 30$

3. $a = 16$, $b =$ _____, $c = 34$

4. $a = 24$, $b = 45$, $c =$ _____

5.

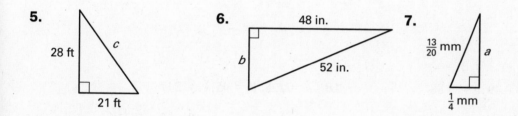

6.   48 in.   **7.**

**Use the converse of the Pythagorean theorem to determine whether the
triangle with the given side lengths is a right triangle.**

8. $a = 24$, $b = 10$, $c = 26$

9. $a = 34$, $b = 44$, $c = 48$

10. $a = 17$, $b = 23$, $c = 29$

11. $a = 54$, $b = 72$, $c = 90$

9.3 Continued **Practice**

For use with pages 442–447

Find the unknown length. Round to the nearest hundredth, if necessary.

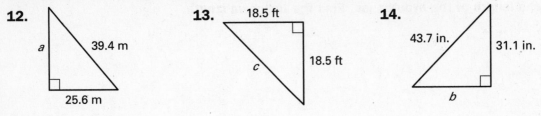

12. a 39.4 m 25.6 m

13. 18.5 ft c 18.5 ft

14. 43.7 in. 31.1 in. b

Determine whether the triangle with the given side lengths is a right triangle.

15. $a = 0.36, b = 0.48, c = 0.60$

16. $a = 1.27, b = 3.46, c = 4.55$

17. $a = 7.56, b = 8.49, c = 9.88$

18. $a = 228, b = 95, c = 247$

19. To get sheets of drywall into a house, construction workers carry the sheets diagonally through an opening. The opening is 36 inches wide by 77 inches tall. What is the widest piece of drywall that can be passed through the opening?

Let a and b represent the lengths of the legs of a right triangle, and let c represent the length of the hypotenuse. Find the unknown length.

20. $a = 2.1, b = 2.8, c = $ _____

21. $a = $ _____, $b = 120, c = 312$

22. $a = 18.5, b = $ _____, $c = 48.1$

23. $a = $ _____, $b = 1, c = \sqrt{2}$

Lesson 9.3

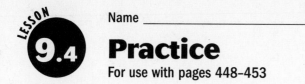

LESSON 9.4

Practice

For use with pages 448–453

Find the perimeter of the triangle. Round to the nearest tenth, if necessary.

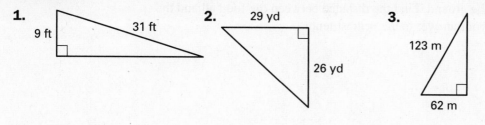

1. 9 ft   31 ft

2. 29 yd   26 yd

3. 123 m   62 m

Let *a* and *b* represent the lengths of the legs of a right triangle, and let *c* represent the length of the hypotenuse. Find the unknown length. Then find the area and perimeter. Round to the nearest tenth, if necessary.

4. $a = 9$ ft, $b = 40$ ft, $c = $ ____

5. $a = 18$ mm, $b = $ ____, $c = 30$ mm

6. $a = $ ____, $b = 48$ in., $c = 52$ in.

7. $a = 48$ yd, $b = 63$ yd, $c = $ ____

8. $a = 102$ ft, $b = 105$ ft, $c = $ ____

9. $a = 0.8$ mm, $b = $ ____, $c = 1.7$ mm

Determine whether the numbers form a Pythagorean triple.

10. 80, 192, 208

11. 15, 48, 52

12. 19, 22, 26

13. 32, 37, 53

Middle School Math, Course 3 **127**
Chapter 9   Practice Workbook

Lesson 9.4

Name _____ Date _____

Practice

For use with pages 448–453

14. A kicker is about to attempt a field goal in a football game. The distance from the football to the goal post is 120 feet. The crossbar of the goal post is 10 feet above the ground. Find the distance between the football and the crossbar. Round your answer to the nearest tenth.

Find the perimeter of the right triangle given its area and the length of one leg.

15. $a = 12$ m
Area $= 60$ m^2

16. $a = 5.6$ ft
Area $= 33.6$ ft^2

17. $a = 9.3$ in.
Area $= 40.92$ in.^{2}

18. Your uncle wants to plant grass. The area in which he wants to plant the grass is in the shape of a right triangle. One side of the triangle is 128 feet long, and the hypotenuse is 272 feet long. Find the area of the triangle. If a bag of grass seed can cover 5000 square feet, how many bags are needed?

Find the value of x.

19.

20.

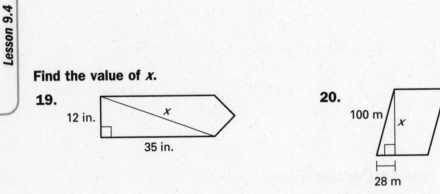

Lesson 9.4

LESSON 9.5

Practice

For use with pages 456–460

Find the value of each variable. Give the exact answer(s).

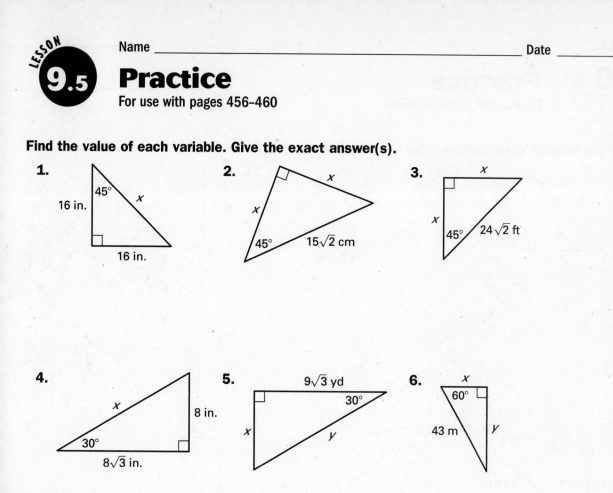

1.

16 in. 45° x

16 in.

2.

x

45° 15√2 cm x

3.

x

x 45° 24√2 ft

4.

x

30°

8√3 in. 8 in.

5.

9√3 yd 30°

x

y

6.

x 60°

43 m y

7. The hypotenuse of a 30°-60°-90° right triangle is 10√3 centimeters. Find the length of the longer leg.

8. A table is in the shape of a square with a side length of 4.08 feet. Draw a diagram of the table. Find the length of the diagonal of the table.

Name _____ Date _____

Practice

For use with pages 456–460

Find the value of each variable. Give the exact answer(s).

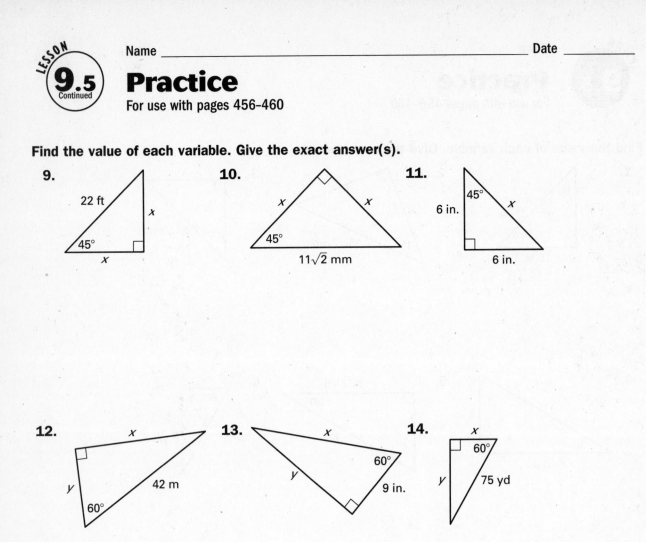

9.

22 ft

x

45°

x

10.

x   x

45°

11√2 mm

11.

45°

6 in.   x

6 in.

12.

x

42 m

y

60°

13.

x

60°

y

9 in.

14.

x   60°

y   75 yd

15. From an observation tower, a forest ranger spots a bear at a
45° angle from his line of vision. His eye level is 36 meters
above ground level. Find the distance between the forest
ranger and the bear. Give an exact answer.

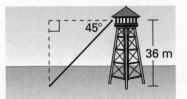

45°

36 m

Name _____ Date _____

Practice

For use with pages 461–469

In △ABC, write the sine, cosine, and tangent ratios for ∠A and ∠B.

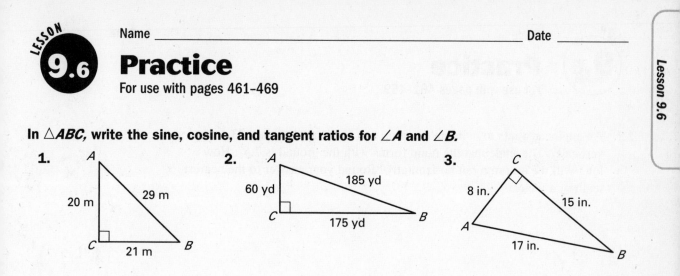

1.

2.

3.

Use a calculator to approximate the given expression. Round your answer to four decimal places.

4. tan 21°   **5.** cos 49°   **6.** sin 83°   **7.** sin 36°

Find the value of x. Round your answer to the nearest hundredth.

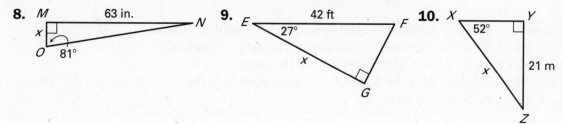

8.   9.   10.

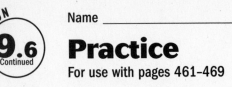

Practice

For use with pages 461–469

11. An engineer wants to build an on-ramp to a highway that rises 23.4 meters vertically. The angle that the ramp forms with the ground is 7.5°. How long will the on-ramp run horizontally? Round your answer to the nearest tenth of a meter.

Find the value of the unknown angle and side. Then write three trigonometric ratios for ∠G.

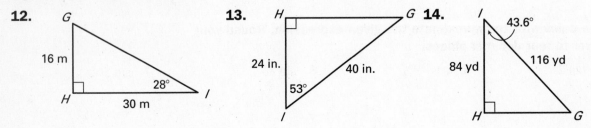

12. G, 16 m, H, 30 m, 28°, I

13. H, 24 in., 53°, 40 in., G, I

14. I, 43.6°, 84 yd, 116 yd, H, G

15. An airplane flying at an altitude of 32,000 feet is headed toward an airport. To guide the airplane to a safe landing, the airport's landing system sends radar signals from the runway to the airplane at a 10° angle above the runway. Measured along the ground, how far is the airplane from the airport runway to the nearest foot?

Name _____ Date _____

LESSON 10.1 Practice

For use with pages 481–485

Find the area of the parallelogram.

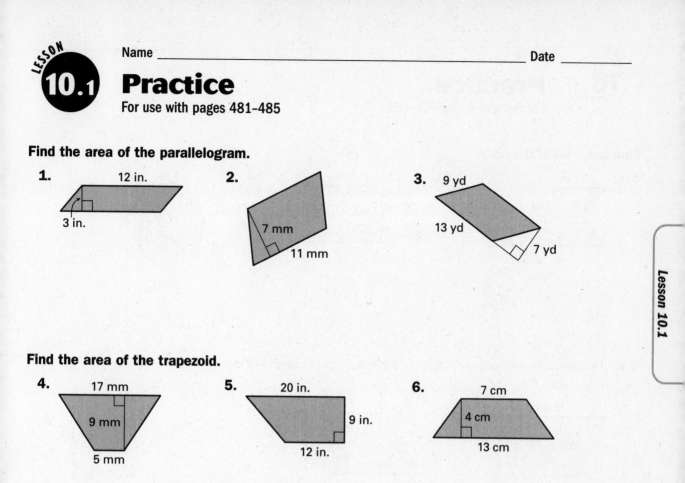

1.   12 in.

3 in.

2.   7 mm

11 mm

3.   9 yd

13 yd

7 yd

Find the area of the trapezoid.

4.   17 mm

9 mm

5 mm

5.   20 in.

9 in.

12 in.

6.   7 cm

4 cm

13 cm

Sketch the figure. Then use an area formula to find the unknown dimension.

7. A parallelogram has an area of 92 square units. Its height is 4 units. Find the base.

8. A trapezoid has an area of 105 square units. Its bases are 12 units and 18 units. Find the height.

9. A trapezoid has an area of 90 square units. It has a base of 4 units and a height of 9 units. Find the other base.

LESSON 10.1 Continued

Practice

For use with pages 481–485

Find the area of the figure.

10.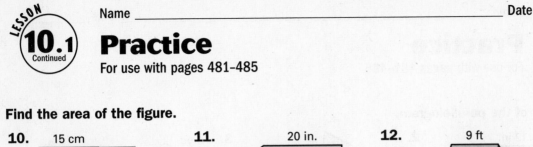
15 cm
7 cm
7 cm

11.
20 in.
14 in.
8 in.
20 in.

12.
9 ft
7 ft
7 ft
15 ft

Lesson 10.1

13. The parallelogram and the trapezoid have the same area. Find the value of *x*.

18 mm
9 mm
x

14 mm
9 mm

Name _____ Date _____

Practice

For use with pages 486–491

Lesson 10.2

Find the area of the circle. Use 3.14 for π.

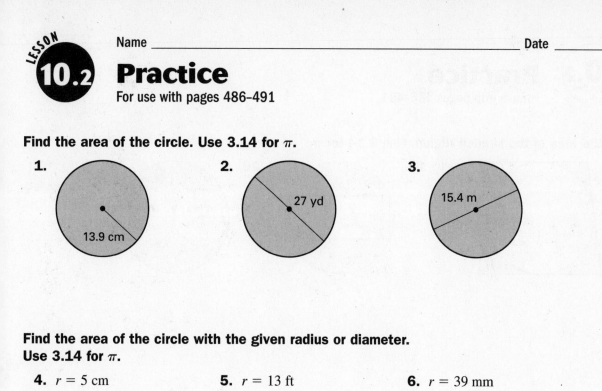

1.

13.9 cm

2.

27 yd

3.

15.4 m

Find the area of the circle with the given radius or diameter.
Use 3.14 for π.

4. $r = 5$ cm

5. $r = 13$ ft

6. $r = 39$ mm

7. $d = 16$ m

8. $d = 24$ yd

9. $d = 60$ in.

Find the radius of the circle with the given area. Use 3.14 for π.

10. $A = 28.26$ mm^2

11. $A = 78.5$ ft^2

12. $A = 254.34$ in.^{2}

13. $A = 379.94$ cm^2

14. $A = 706.5$ m^2

15. $A = 18.0864$ yd^2

16. The circle at the center of a soccer field has a diameter of 20 feet. Find the area of the circle. Use 3.14 for π.

17. The St. Peter's Basilica dome in Rome, Italy, could cover a ground area of 1365 square meters. Find the diameter of the dome. Use 3.14 for π.

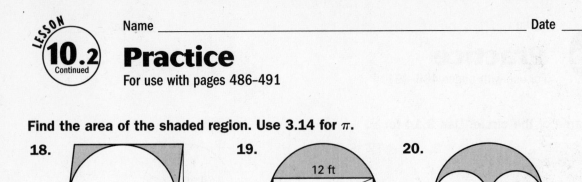

LESSON
10.2 **Practice**
Continued
For use with pages 486–491

Find the area of the shaded region. Use 3.14 for π.

18.

16 m

16 m

19.

12 ft

5 ft

20.

4 in.   4 in.

Write and solve an equation to find the radius of the circle given its circumference C. Use the radius to find the area of the circle. Use 3.14 for π.

21. $C = 50.24$ in.   **22.** $C = 94.2$ m   **23.** $C = 150.72$ cm

24. If the area of a circle is 81π square yards, what is the radius?

25. A square with a perimeter of 16 inches is inscribed in a circle.
What is the area not occupied by the square? (*Hint*: Find the
diameter of the circle by using a special triangle.) Use 3.14 for π.

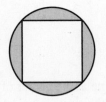

Name _____ Date _____

Practice

For use with pages 492–495

Classify the solid. Then tell whether it is a polyhedron.

1. 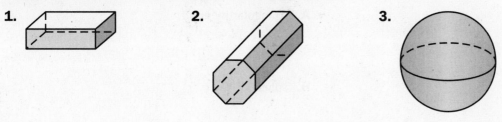   2.   3.

Show two ways to represent the solid. Then count the number of faces, edges, and vertices.

4. octagonal pyramid   5. pentagonal prism

Match the description with the solid.

6. 2 circular bases   **A.** triangular pyramid

7. 4 faces   **B.** cylinder

8. 6 faces   **C.** rectangular prism

Lesson 10.3

Name _____ Date _____

Practice

For use with pages 492–495

Match the number of vertices with the solid.

9. 0   **A.** triangular pyramid

10. 4   **B.** sphere

11. 10   **C.** pentagonal prism

Identify the solid from the top, front, and side views.

12. Top   Front   Side

13. Top   Front   Side

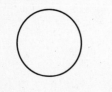

Identify the solids that form the object.

14.   15.

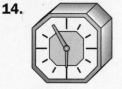

Lesson 10.3

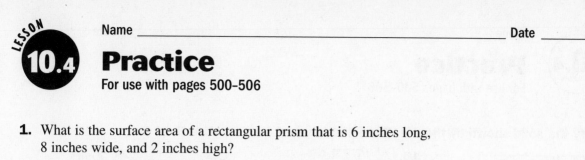

LESSON 10.4

Practice

For use with pages 500–506

1. What is the surface area of a rectangular prism that is 6 inches long, 8 inches wide, and 2 inches high?

    A. 14 in.^{2} **B.** 52 in.^{2} **C.** 96 in.^{2} **D.** 152 in.^{2}

Find the surface area of the prism, where *B* is the area of the base, *P* is the perimeter of the base, and *h* is the height.

2. $B = 8$ m^2, $P = 3$ m, $h = 6$ m   **3.** $B = 15$ in.^{2}, $P = 12$ in., $h = 3$ in.

4. $B = 42$ yd^2, $P = 23$ yd, $h = 8$ yd   **5.** $B = 58$ mm^2, $P = 36$ m, $h = 20$ m

Sketch a cylinder with radius *r* and height *h*. Then find its surface area. Use 3.14 for π.

6. $r = 4$ cm, $h = 8$ cm   **7.** $r = 10$ in., $h = 12$ in.   **8.** $r = 3$ ft, $h = 21$ ft

Name _____ Date _____

Practice

For use with pages 500–506

Identify the solid shown by the net. Then find the surface area. Use 3.14 for π.

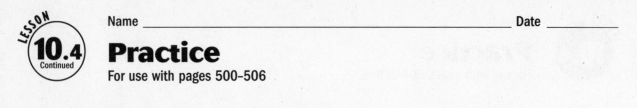

9.

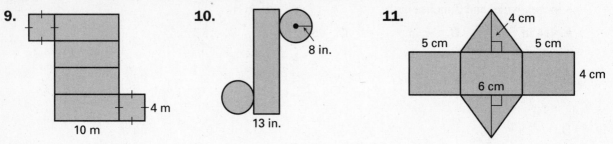

10 m   4 m

10.

8 in.

13 in.

11.

4 cm

5 cm   5 cm

6 cm   4 cm

Draw a net for the solid. Then find the surface area of the solid. Use 3.14 for π.

12.   15 in.   2 in.

13.   10 m

8 m

8 m

6 m

14.   6 ft

4 ft

13 ft

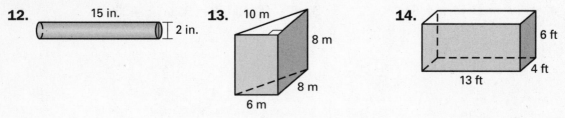

Find the surface area of the solid. Use 3.14 for π.

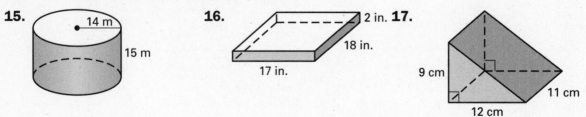

15.   14 m   15 m

16.   2 in.   18 in.

17 in.

17.   9 cm   11 cm   12 cm

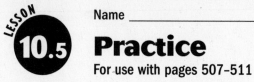

10.5 **Practice**

For use with pages 507–511

Find the surface area of the square pyramid with base side length *s* and slant height ℓ.

1. $s = 4$ m
  $\ell = 13$ m

2. $s = 8$ in.
  $\ell = 15$ in.

3. $s = 11$ cm
  $\ell = 17.3$ cm

4. $s = 18$ yd
  $\ell = 14.1$ yd

Find the surface area of the cone with radius *r* and slant height ℓ. Use 3.14 for π.

5. $r = 6$ m
  $\ell = 9$ m

6. $r = 10$ in.
  $\ell = 15$ in.

7. $r = 13$ cm
  $\ell = 9.6$ cm

8. $r = 24$ yd
  $\ell = 8.2$ yd

Sketch a net for the solid. Then find the surface area. Round to the nearest tenth.

9.

10.

11.

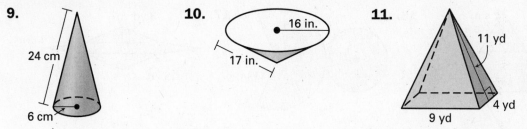

LESSON 10.5 Continued

Practice

For use with pages 507–511

Find the surface area of the solid. Round to the nearest tenth.

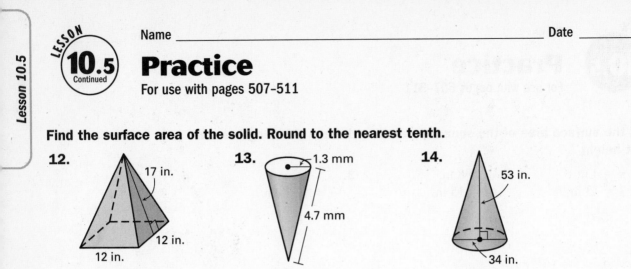

12. 17 in. 12 in. 12 in.

13. 1.3 mm 4.7 mm

14. 53 in. 34 in.

Find the surface area of the solid represented by the net. Round to the nearest tenth.

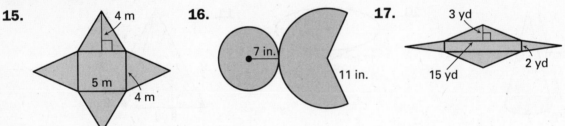

15. 4 m 5 m 4 m

16. 7 in. 11 in.

17. 3 yd 15 yd 2 yd

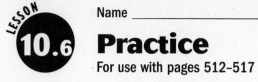
Practice

For use with pages 512–517

Find the volume of the rectangular prism with length l, width w, and height h.

1. $l = 5$ m, $w = 8$ m, $h = 9$ m

2. $l = 10$ in., $w = 14$ in., $h = 15$ in.

3. $l = 16$ yd, $w = 10.2$ yd, $h = 4.3$ yd

4. $l = 12$ mm, $w = 17$ mm, $h = 2\frac{1}{2}$ mm

Find the volume of the cylinder with radius r and height h. Use 3.14 for π.

5. $r = 6$ in., $h = 12$ in.

6. $r = 2$ cm, $h = 13$ cm

7. $r = 1.9$ m, $h = 8.7$ m

Find the volume of the solid. If two units of measure are used, give your answer in the smaller units. Round your answer to the nearest hundredth.

8.

7 mm
4 mm
13 mm

9.

8 ft
21 ft

10.

17 m
29 m
21 m

Name _____ Date _____

Practice

For use with pages 512–517

Find the volume of the solid. If two units of measure are used, give your answer in the smaller units. Round your answer to the nearest hundredth.

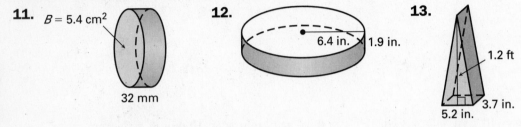

11. $B = 5.4$ cm^2

32 mm

12. 6.4 in. 1.9 in.

13. 1.2 ft 3.7 in. 5.2 in.

Find the volume of the solid. Round your answer to the nearest hundredth.

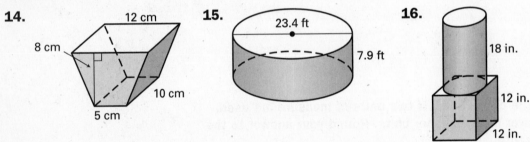

14. 12 cm 8 cm 10 cm 5 cm

15. 23.4 ft 7.9 ft

16. 18 in. 12 in. 12 in. 12 in.

Name _____ Date _____

Practice

For use with pages 518–523

Find the volume of the pyramid with base area *B* and height *h*.

1. $B = 18 \text{ in.}^2, h = 5$ in.

2. $B = 6.3 \text{ mm}^2, h = 2.9$ mm

Find the volume of the pyramid.

3.

4.

5.

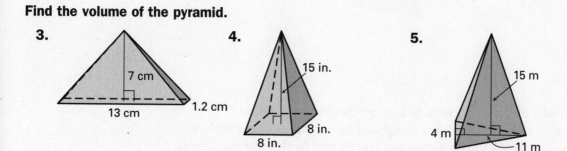

Find the volume of the square pyramid with base side length *s* and height *h*.

6. $s = 3$ in., $h = 7$ in.

7. $s = 9$ mm, $h = 14$ mm

8. $s = 9$ ft, $h = \dfrac{1}{2}$ ft

Name _____ Date _____

Practice

For use with pages 518–523

Find the volume of the cone. If two units of measure are used, give your answer in the smaller units. Round to the nearest tenth.

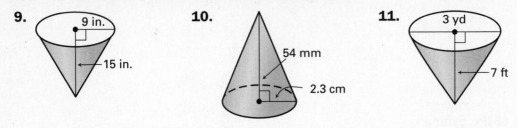

9. 9 in. 15 in.

10. 54 mm 2.3 cm

11. 3 yd 7 ft

Find the volume of the cone with the given dimensions, where r = radius, d = diameter, and h = height. If two units of measure are used, give your answer in the smaller units. Round to the nearest tenth.

12. $r = 4$ in., $h = 12$ in.   **13.** $r = 2.1$ m, $h = 84$ cm   **14.** $d = 11$ ft, $h = 24$ ft

Find the volume of the pyramid with the given height and the base shown. Round to the nearest tenth.

15. $h = 2.7$ in.

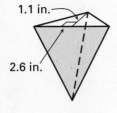

1.1 in.

2.6 in.

16. $h = 15$ m

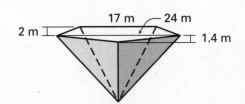

2 m   17 m   24 m   1.4 m

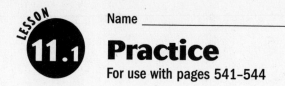

LESSON 11.1 Practice

For use with pages 541–544

Complete the statement.

1. A relation is a set of ordered pairs that relates an _____ to an _____.

2. A relation is a function if for each input there is exactly _____ output.

3. The _____ of a function is the set of all possible input values.

4. The _____ of a function is the set of all possible output values.

5. The function rule assigns each number in the _____ to exactly one number in the _____.

Decide whether the relation is a function.

6. $(3, 2)$, $(3, 8)$, $(-2, -3)$, $(0, 7)$, $(-1, 5)$, $(-4, 2)$, $(-3, -7)$

7. $(4, 4)$, $(3, 2)$, $(-1, 0)$, $(0, 5)$, $(1, -2)$, $(6, 3)$, $(1, -7)$

8.

Input	4	2	−2	1
Output	1	3	2	4

9.

Input	−1	−3	0	−3
Output	5	3	0	2

Make an input-output table for the function rule. Use a domain of −2, −1, 0, 1, and 2. Identify the range.

10. $y = 2x - 1$ 11. $y = x^2 + 3$ 12. $y = \frac{1}{4}x + 1$ 13. $y = -3x - 7$

Name _____ Date _____

Practice

For use with pages 541–544

In Exercises 14 and 15, write a function rule that relates *x* and *y*.

14.

Input *x*	1	2	3	4
Output *y*	7	12	17	22

15.

Input *x*	1	3	5	7
Output *y*	2	4	6	8

16. You go out for dinner with four friends. Each person orders a meal that is the same price. Is the price of the entire meal a function of the number of dinners purchased? Explain.

17. Jose is mowing lawns to earn some money. He gets $15 for every lawn that he mows. Some lawns take twice as long as others. Is the amount of money he earns a function of the time he spends mowing lawns?

Write a function rule that relates *r* and *t*.

18.

Input *r*	1	2	3	4
Output *t*	11	25	39	53

19.

Input *r*	0	1	2	3
Output *t*	4	12	20	28

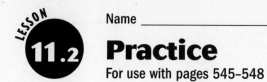

Name _____ Date _____

Practice
For use with pages 545–548

Complete the statement.

1. A _____ plot is the graph of a collection of ordered pairs.

2. In a positive relationship, the *y*-coordinates tend to _____ as the *x*-coordinates _____.

3. In a negative relationship, the *y*-coordinates tend to _____ as the *x*-coordinates _____.

4. When there is no relationship, no _____ exists between the coordinates.

Make a scatter plot of the data. What conclusions can you make?

5.

Game	Points Scored
1	8
2	11
3	13
4	17

6.

Discount	Price
$10	$55
$20	$45
$30	$35

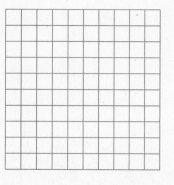

7.

Age in Years	12	8	13	10	9
Number of Pets	4	3	2	0	2

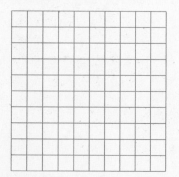

Lesson 11.2

Name _____ Date _____

11.2 **Practice**

For use with pages 545–548

Make a scatter plot of the data. Describe the relationship between the variables. Use the relationship to find the next ordered pair.

8.

x	1	2	3	4	5
y	3	1	−1	−3	

9.

x	3	4	5	6	7
y	34	43	51	59	

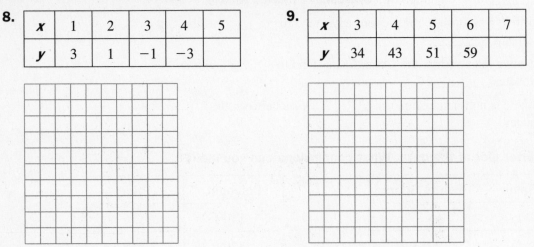

In Exercises 10–12, what type of relationship might you expect for the given data?

10. the size of a television screen and the number of channels on the television

11. the length of the side of a square and the perimeter of the square

12. the number of grades of school completed and the number of grades left until high school graduation

13. Make a table showing the whole number values of length and width of a rectangle whose perimeter is 14 inches. Make a scatter plot of the data. Draw a line that shows the overall pattern of the data. Predict the width of the rectangle when the length is 4.5 inches.

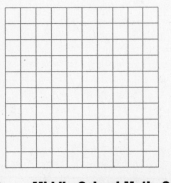

Lesson 11.2

Name _____ Date _____

Practice

For use with pages 549–553

Copy and complete the table for the equation.

x	−7	0	7	14
y				

1. $y = x + 11$ **2.** $y = 13 - 3x$ **3.** $y = -15 - 2x$

Tell whether the ordered pair is a solution of the equation.

4. $y = 5x - 3$; $(4, 16)$ **5.** $y = -3x + 1$; $(0, -1)$ **6.** $y = 9 - x$; $(-2, 11)$

7. $y = 12 - 7x$; $(5, -2)$ **8.** $y = \frac{1}{3}x + 2$; $(9, 5)$ **9.** $y = 6x - 30$; $(7, 12)$

List four solutions of the equation.

10. $y = 2x + 6$ **11.** $y = -5 - 4x$ **12.** $y = \frac{1}{2}x + 3$

13. $y = 24 - 7x$ **14.** $y = \frac{5}{8}x + 1$ **15.** $y = \frac{1}{3}x - 8$

In Exercises 16–19, tell whether the ordered pair is a solution of the equation.

16. $3x - y = 19.6$; $(2.46, 9.38)$ **17.** $7x + y = 23.8$; $(1.5, 13.3)$

18. $x + 5y = 35.14$; $(17.37, 3.554)$ **19.** $3x - 4y = -16.25$; $(1.76, -5.49)$

Name _____ Date _____

Practice
For use with pages 549–553

20. You want to buy a new bike. You have $50 in your savings account. You earn $12 for every lawn that you mow. Use the equation $B = 50 + 12m$, where B is the total cost of the bike and m is the number of lawns that you need to mow. If the total cost of the bike is $165, how many lawns will you need to mow if you want to purchase the bike?

In Exercises 21 and 22, write an equation in two variables for the values in the table.

21.

x	-1	0	1	2
y	-2	1	4	7

22.

x	1	3	5	7
y	2	-4	-10	-16

23. Estimate the values of $4x$ and $12y$ to explain why $\left(\dfrac{9}{8}, \dfrac{-5}{6}\right)$ is *not* a solution of $4x + 12y = 15$.

LESSON 11.4

Name _____ Date _____

Practice

For use with pages 554–561

Match the equation with the description of its graph.

1. $x = -3$
          2. $y = 8$
          3. $y = x - 4$

A. vertical line
          B. horizontal line
          C. slanted line

Make a table of values for the equation.

4. $3x - y = 7$
          5. $y - 4 = 0$
          6. $-2x + 5y = 9$

Find three ordered pairs that are solutions of the given equation.

7. $y = x + 8$
          8. $y = 4x - 5$
          9. $y = -3$

Tell whether the equation is a linear equation.

10. $3x + 4y = 10$
          11. $6x - 9y = -4$
          12. $5x^2 + 2y = 6$

Graph the linear equation.

13. $y = x + 7$
          14. $y = x - 6$
          15. $y = x - 14$

16. $y = 5x + 5$
          17. $y = 8x$
          18. $y = -2x + 13$

19. $y = 20 - 4x$
          20. $y = \frac{1}{4}x + 5$
          21. $y = -\frac{2}{5}x + 16$

Lesson 11.4

Name _____ Date _____

Practice
For use with pages 554–561

22. $y = 6$

23. $x = -4$

24. $x = 15$

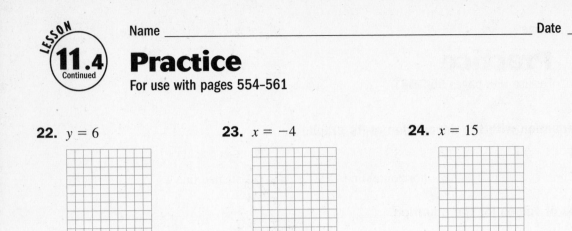

In Exercises 25 and 26, write the equation of the line.

25.

26.

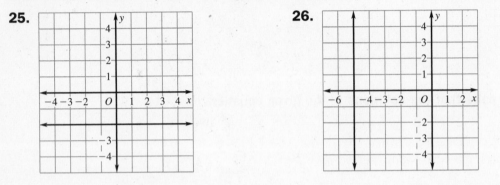

27. Graph the lines $x = 5$ and $y = -2$ in the same coordinate plane. Write the coordinates of the point where the lines intersect. Explain how you can find the coordinates of this point without graphing. Tell what the intersection point of the lines $x = -7$ and $y = -6$ would be.

28. Your new minivan gets 20 miles per gallon of gasoline. The minivan already had 43 miles on the odometer when you bought it. You can determine the number of miles the minivan has been driven by using the equation $M = 20g + 43$, where M is the total number of miles and g is the number of gallons of gasoline used since you bought the minivan. Graph the equation and then estimate how many miles the minivan will have been driven after 4 gallons of gasoline are used.

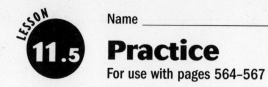

Name _____ Date _____

11.5 Practice

For use with pages 564–567

Identify the *x*-intercept and the *y*-intercept.

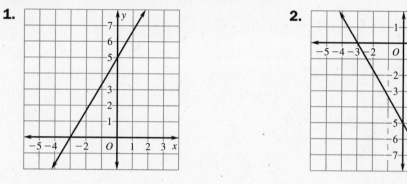

1.

2.

Find the intercepts of the graph of the equation.

3. $y = 3x - 6$ **4.** $y = -4x + 16$ **5.** $y = 9x + 27$

6. $x + 5y = -4$ **7.** $7x + 3y = 21$ **8.** $2x - 3y = 12$

9. $-x + 6y = 20$ **10.** $12x - 15y = 18$ **11.** $15y - 3x = 6$

Graph the line that has the given intercepts.

12. *x*-intercept: 5   **13.** *x*-intercept: -3 **14.** *x*-intercept: 6
   y-intercept: -2 *y*-intercept: 7   *y*-intercept: 4

Find the intercepts of the graph of the equation.

15. $y = 3$ **16.** $y = -8$ **17.** $x = 12$ **18.** $x = -9$

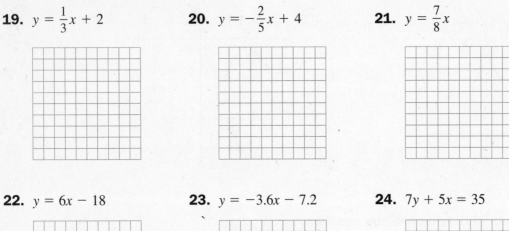

11.5 Practice
Continued

For use with pages 564–567

Graph the equation using intercepts.

19. $y = \frac{1}{3}x + 2$

20. $y = -\frac{2}{5}x + 4$

21. $y = \frac{7}{8}x$

22. $y = 6x - 18$

23. $y = -3.6x - 7.2$

24. $7y + 5x = 35$

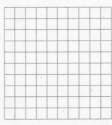

In Exercises 25–30, find the intercepts of the graph of the equation. Round to the nearest hundredth.

25. $y = -1.56x + 2.85$

26. $y = 3.09x - 8.7$

27. $y = -7.21x - 18.94$

28. $3.4x + 2.5y = 1.6$

29. $10.2y - 3.7x = 15.45$

30. $8.8y + 2.9x = 6.4$

31. What kind of line has only an x-intercept?

32. Peyton earns \$12 an hour working at a grocery store. He also earns \$15 an hour helping his brother in the moving business. He wants to earn \$240 a week between the two jobs. The equation $12g + 15m = 240$ models the situation. Find the intercepts of the graph of the equation. What do they represent?

33. If the x-intercept of a line is positive and the y-intercept is positive, then does the line slant up or down from left to right? Explain your reasoning.

Name _____ Date _____

Practice

For use with pages 568–574

Match each line with the given type of slope.

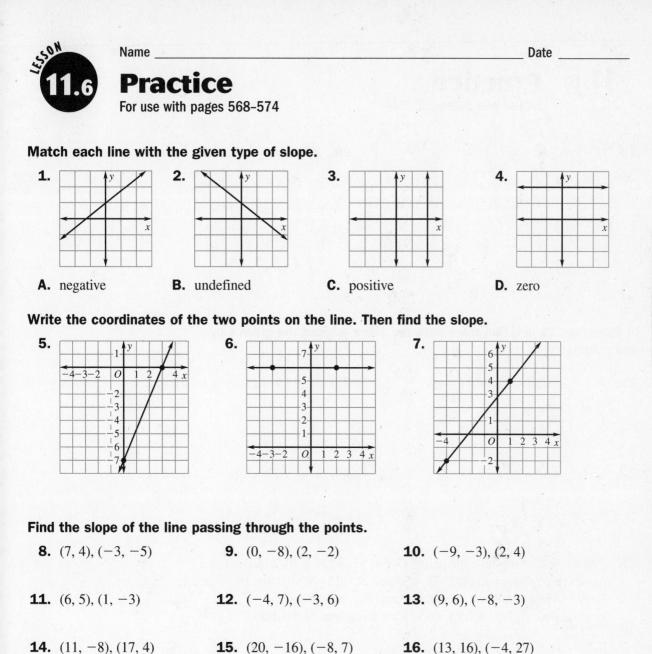

A. negative   **B.** undefined   **C.** positive   **D.** zero

Write the coordinates of the two points on the line. Then find the slope.

Find the slope of the line passing through the points.

8. $(7, 4), (-3, -5)$

9. $(0, -8), (2, -2)$

10. $(-9, -3), (2, 4)$

11. $(6, 5), (1, -3)$

12. $(-4, 7), (-3, 6)$

13. $(9, 6), (-8, -3)$

14. $(11, -8), (17, 4)$

15. $(20, -16), (-8, 7)$

16. $(13, 16), (-4, 27)$

The three points are vertices of a triangle. Plot and connect the points.
Then find the slope of each side of the triangle.

17. $A(0, 0), B(-4, 0), C(0, -8)$

18. $E(6, -5), F(1, 3), G(-4, 0)$

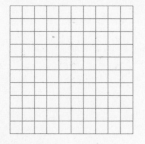

Name _____ Date _____

Practice
For use with pages 568–574

19. $L(-5, 8), M(-2, 1), N(1, -3)$

20. $X(10, 6), Y(2, 3), Z(12, -1)$

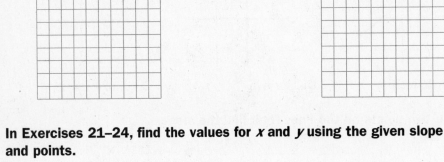

In Exercises 21–24, find the values for *x* and *y* using the given slope and points.

21. $m = \dfrac{1}{4}$ and $(0, 0), (x, 4), (3, y)$

22. $m = 3$ and $(1, -4), (x, 5), (-2, y)$

23. $m = \dfrac{5}{3}$ and $(3, 7), (x, 2), (-3, y)$

24. $m = -7$ and $(2, -2) (x, -37), (-2, y)$

25. One line passes through the points $G(-1, 5)$ and $H(2, 9)$. A second line passes through the points $X(-3, -2)$ and $Y(5, 12)$. Which line has a greater slope? Explain how you can tell by graphing the two lines.
Explain how you can tell by calculating the slopes of the lines.

26. A line contains the points (x, y) and $(x - 3, y + 4)$. Find the slope of the line.

27. Describe what a line with an undefined slope looks like. Describe what a line with a slope of zero looks like.

Lesson 11.6

Name _____ Date _____

Practice

For use with pages 575–580

Rewrite the equation in slope-intercept form.

1. $5x - y = 8$

2. $-11x + y = 13$

3. $7x + 2y = 12$

Match the equation with its graph.

4. $y = 3x + 4$

5. $y = -3x + 4$

6. $y = \frac{1}{3}x + 4$

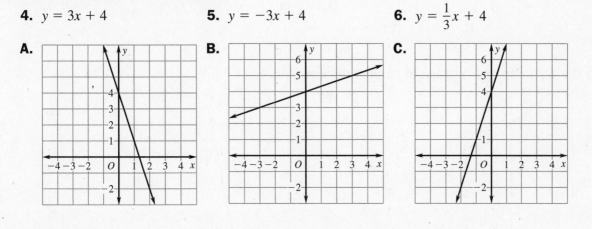

A. B. C.

Find the slope and y-intercept of the equation. Then graph the equation.

7. $y = x + 9$

8. $y = \frac{1}{5}x - 2$

9. $y = -5x + 1$

10. $y = -x + \frac{6}{11}$

11. $y = 7$

12. $y = \frac{3}{4}x$

Name _____ Date _____

Practice

For use with pages 575–580

Rewrite the equation in slope-intercept form. Then find the slope and *y*-intercept of the line.

13. $y = 14 - 2x$

14. $y + 8 = 4x$

15. $y - \dfrac{3}{5}x = 0$

16. $6x - 3y = 15$

17. $\dfrac{1}{8}x - y = 7$

18. $15x - 10y = 32$

Write the equation of the graph in slope-intercept form.

19.

20.

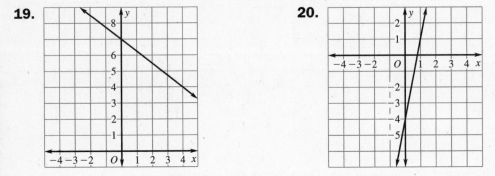

Name _____ Date _____

Practice

For use with pages 583–588

Tell whether the point is a solution of the inequality.

1. $7x - 3y < 10$; $(4, 5)$

2. $x - 5y \geq 16$; $(5, -3)$

3. $-4x + 10y \leq 25$; $(2, 1)$

4. $6y + 3x > 18$; $(-5, 4)$

Match the inequality with its graph.

5. $y < 2x + 7$

6. $y > 2x + 7$

7. $y \geq 2x + 7$

8. $y \leq 2x + 7$

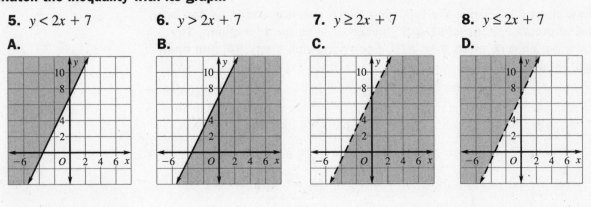

A.   B.   C.   D.

Graph the inequality.

9. $y < x + 7$

10. $y > 3x - 5$

11. $y \geq 12 - 4x$

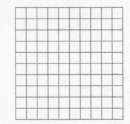

12. $y \leq 6x + 3$

13. $y > 7x + 15$

14. $y \geq -2x - 11$

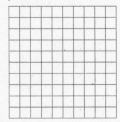

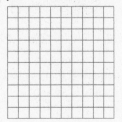

15. $5x \leq 30$

16. $48 > 6x$

17. $8y < -24$

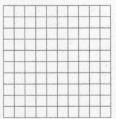

LESSON 11.8 Continued

Practice

For use with pages 583–588

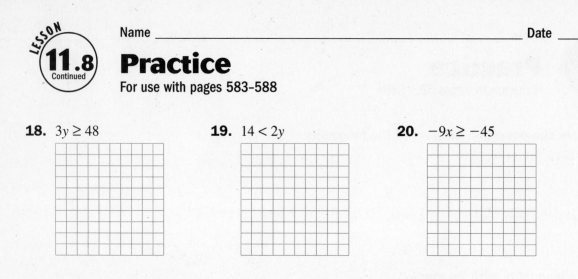

18. $3y \geq 48$

19. $14 < 2y$

20. $-9x \geq -45$

In Exercises 21–23, use the following. Jim's catering business has been hired to prepare sandwiches and glasses of juice for a luncheon. The meal must cost no more than $76. Each sandwich costs $4, and each glass of juice costs $2.

21. The inequality $4x + 2y \leq 76$ models the situation, where x is the number of sandwiches ordered and y is the number of glasses of juice ordered. How many sandwiches can Jim prepare if he prepares 20 glasses of juice?

22. Graph the inequality.

23. Use the graph to find the maximum number of glasses of juice that can be used if Jim prepares 13 sandwiches.

24. Write the inequality that represents the half-plane that is not the solution of the inequality $4x + 2y \geq 5$.

25. Write an inequality for which the graph has a dotted line.

12.1 Practice

For use with pages 597–600

Make an ordered stem-and-leaf plot of the data. Identify the interval that includes the most data values.

1. 53, 61, 68, 42, 93, 72, 65, 40

2. 8, 6, 15, 37, 22, 19, 27, 5, 33

3. 124, 129, 135, 148, 168, 152, 122

4. 301, 325, 348, 322, 316, 309, 335, 327, 306

5. 23.4, 21.9, 20.1, 26.3, 23.8, 21.7, 21.3

6. 9.2, 8.4, 7.3, 9.3, 10.3, 4.1, 8.5, 9.7, 6.8

7. The stem-and-leaf plot shows the heights, in inches, of a group of three-year olds. What are the tallest and shortest heights? Which interval has the fewest number of heights?

```
2 | 3 6
3 | 2 4 5 6 8 8
4 | 0 1 2 6 7
5 | 0           Key: 3 | 2 = 32
```

8. The data show the number of minutes it takes 14 people to commute to work. Make an ordered stem-and-leaf plot. What is the range of commute times? Do the commuters usually spend more or less than 25 minutes traveling?

15, 24, 29, 33, 37, 16, 26, 38, 45, 8, 13, 19, 26, 34

Name _____ Date _____

Practice

For use with pages 597–600

Make a double stem-and-leaf plot of the two sets of data.

9. Set A: 26, 34, 39, 48, 56, 31, 35
  Set B: 24, 29, 23, 35, 38, 41, 19, 26

10. Set C: 53, 56, 92, 81, 72, 62, 92, 52
  Set D: 62, 63, 74, 63, 68, 71, 82, 69

11. The two sets of data below represent the miles per gallon of gasoline
two different types of cars are able to get on the highway. Make an ordered
double stem-and-leaf plot of the data. Describe the relationship between the
mileage of the two different types of cars.

  SUV: 19, 21, 16, 22, 17

  Sedan: 24, 30, 23, 31, 28

**In Exercises 12–14, use the data that show the average length of eight
front porches in inches (*I*).**

  60, 73, 85, 65, 92, 81, 76, 92

12. Make an ordered stem-and-leaf plot of the data. What is the range?

13. Convert the data to centimeters (*C*) using the formula $C = 2.54I$. Round
to the nearest unit.

14. Make an ordered stem-and-leaf plot of the converted data. Compare
the two plots. In what ways are they different? Explain.

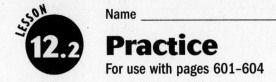
Complete the statement.

1. The least data value of a data set is the _____ extreme and the greatest data value of a data set is the _____ extreme.

Make a box-and-whisker plot of the data.

2. 15 mm, 19 mm, 25 mm, 34 mm, 28 mm, 32 mm, 16 mm, 26 mm

3. 4 h, 7 h, 11 h, 3 h, 18 h, 23 h

4. 260 g, 170 g, 163 g, 242 g, 309 g, 315 g, 115 g, 207 g

5. 62 mph, 71 mph, 45 mph, 25 mph, 32 mph, 57 mph, 52 mph

The box-and-whisker plot shows the number of seconds a song on a CD lasts. Estimate the value.

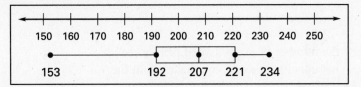

6. range

7. median

8. lower quartile

9. upper quartile

10. lower extreme

11. upper extreme

Lesson 12.2

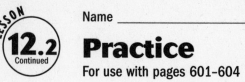
12. Farrah runs every day to train for a marathon. The number of miles she ran
over the last ten days are: 7, 3, 4, 9, 6, 11, 3, 5, 11, and 7. Organize the list
of miles run from least to greatest. Then make a box-and-whisker plot of
the data. What conclusions can you make?

13. The masses, in kilograms, of nine Indian bull elephants are 3145, 3370,
3210, 3197, 3212, 3291, 3087, 3371, and 3347. Make a box-and-whisker
plot of the data. Describe what the plot shows.

14. The box-and-whisker plots show the number of goals scored per soccer
game by two different players. What conclusions can you make about the
two players' performances? Which player is more consistent? Explain.

```
      0    1    2    3    4    5
      ●────┬──┬──────┐────●      Player A
      0    1  1.5    3    4
          ●──┬──┬───┐──●         Player B
          1 1.5  2   3   4
```

Lesson 12.2

Name _____ Date _____

Practice

For use with pages 605–611

Convert the value into an angle measure for display in a circle graph.

1. 25%   **2.** $\frac{3}{8}$ **3.** 30 out of 75   **4.** 18%

In Exercises 5 and 6, use the table that shows the numbers of marching band members from each grade.

5. Make a circle graph to display the numbers of marching band members from each grade as a fraction of the total number of marching band members.

Marching Band	
Fourth Grade	30
Fifth Grade	28
Sixth Grade	23
Seventh Grade	36
Eighth Grade	21

6. Every year, each marching band member had to work 8 hours at fund-raising events. Make a bar graph that shows the total number of hours members from each grade worked at fund-raising events.

7. The table shows the number of games won by a baseball team from 1996 to 2002. Make a line graph of the data. Describe the data change over time.

Year	1996	1997	1998	1999	2000	2001	2002
Games won	22	16	21	27	32	35	37

Name _____ Date _____

Practice

For use with pages 605–611

In Exercises 8 and 9, use the table that shows the results of a survey over two school years asking students their favorite subject in school.

Subject	English	History	Math	Science	Other
2001–2002	23.8%	21.7%	21.5%	19.4%	13.6%
2002–2003	17.4%	24.2%	20.7%	23.3%	14.4%

8. Make a circle graph of the data for the school years 2001–2002 and 2002–2003.

9. Which subject had the largest percent increase between the two school years? Which subject had the largest percent decrease?

10. What type of display would you use to display the number of days with precipitation and the type of precipitation that occurred? Explain.

11. What type of display would you use to display the number of inches of precipitation received each day over a month? Explain.

Lesson 12.3

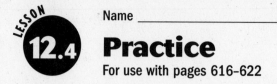

Name _____ Date _____

Practice

For use with pages 616–622

In Exercises 1–4, make a tree diagram to find the number of choices that are possible. Then check your answer using the counting principle.

1. Choose a red, blue, or yellow shirt with khaki or black pants.

2. Choose a scoop of vanilla, chocolate, or strawberry ice cream in a sugar or waffle cone.

3. Choose to run, swim laps, play basketball, or take an aerobics class and go in the sauna or in the hot tub afterwards.

4. Choose to do math, science, or English homework and then read a book, watch television, or play a board game.

5. You and five friends go out to dinner. There are three different entrée choices. You each pick an entrée at random. What is the probability that you all pick the same entrée for dinner?

LESSON
(12.4)
Continued

Practice

For use with pages 616–622

6. The table shows some of the options for a new car. Make a tree diagram to find the number of different ways a person can select a body type, a transmission type, and a color. Then use the counting principle to check your answer.

Body	Transmission	Color
Sedan	Automatic	Red
Sports Car	Manual	Green
SUV		White
		Black

7. In a small city, there are three different exchanges possible for each 7-digit telephone number. The exchange is the first 3 digits of the telephone number. Each of the last 4 digits of the telephone number can be any integer from 0 to 9. How many telephone numbers are possible in the town?

8. Your CD player is set for random play. There are 20 CDs in the player and there are 10 songs on each CD. You have one favorite song on each of the CDs. What is the probability that the next song played is one of them?

9. You have a combination lock that has the numbers 1–40 on the dial. You forgot the combination, but you remember that the combination is three numbers, the last digit of all three numbers is 6, and none of the numbers are between 1 and 10. You make a random guess with what you know. What is the probability that you will get the combination?

10. A coin is tossed 6 times. What is the probability that the results are either all heads or all tails?

Lesson 12.4

12.5 Practice

For use with pages 623–626

Name _____ Date _____

Complete the statement.

1. 7! can be written as ____ × ____ × ____ × ____ × ____ × ____ × ____.

2. $_7P_4$ can be written as $\dfrac{\_\_!}{\_\_!}$.

Match the expression with its value.

3. 3!　　　　　**4.** $_5P_3$　　　　　**5.** $_6P_2$　　　　　**6.** 5!

A. 120　　　　**B.** 60　　　　**C.** 30　　　　**D.** 6

Evaluate.

7. 7!　　　　**8.** 10!　　　　**9.** 8!　　　　**10.** 0!

In Exercises 11–18, find the number of permutations.

11. $_3P_1$　　　　**12.** $_7P_3$　　　　**13.** $_9P_7$　　　　**14.** $_6P_3$

15. $_{11}P_8$　　　　**16.** $_{15}P_4$　　　　**17.** $_{18}P_6$　　　　**18.** $_{21}P_2$

19. At a county fair, a judge must award first, second, and third place for show rabbits. There are 16 rabbits entered in the competition. How many different arrangements are possible?

20. There are 6 ski runs at a ski resort that you want to go down before the end of the day. In how many different orders can you go down the ski runs?

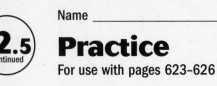

Practice

For use with pages 623–626

21. You need a 4-digit password for the code on the garage door keypad. Write an expression to represent the number of different passwords you could choose. Then write an expression to find the number of passwords you could choose if you can use each number only once.

22. Your friend says that $_6P_4$ is equal to $\dfrac{6!}{4!}$. Is your friend correct? Explain.

23. A bubblegum machine dispenses red, yellow, green, orange, pink, blue, and white pieces of bubblegum. There is only 1 piece of each color left in the machine. If you put two quarters in the machine, you get 2 pieces of bubblegum. Find the number of different orders in which you can get 2 pieces of bubblegum.

24. You have 9 homework assignments to do tonight. In how many different orders can you complete the assignments?

Name _____ Date _____

Practice

For use with pages 627–631

In Exercises 1–12, find the number of combinations.

1. $_5C_2$ **2.** $_6C_3$ **3.** $_9C_2$ **4.** $_{12}C_4$

5. $_8C_4$ **6.** $_{10}C_4$ **7.** $_{11}C_7$ **8.** $_{15}C_9$

9. $_7C_6$ **10.** $_{19}C_{17}$ **11.** $_{25}C_{13}$ **12.** $_{82}C_{80}$

13. Your teacher wants to send 5 students from your social studies class of 28 students to a conference. How many different groups of 5 can be created to go to this conference?

14. How many 4-person committees can be formed from 16 people?

15. How many groups of 3 puppies could be chosen from a litter of 5 puppies?

16. You want to create a pizza with three toppings. There are 8 different toppings to choose from: pepperoni, sausage, ham, onions, mushrooms, green peppers, black olives, and extra cheese. How many different combinations of toppings are there?

LESSON
12.6
Continued

Name _____ Date _____

Practice

For use with pages 627–631

Lesson 12.6

17. Barry wants to plant 5 different types of trees in his yard. The nursery where he purchases the trees has 12 different types of trees. How many combinations of 5 tree types can he choose from?

18. A company with 18 employees has tickets for a basketball game. They want to give some of the tickets to their employees. Draw a diagram or write an expression so that you can determine the number of ways the company can choose 2 employees. Then find the number of ways that the company can choose 3 employees.

In Exercises 19–22, tell whether the possibilities should be counted using a *permutation* or *combination.* Then find the answer.

19. You want to place 2 different colored pillows on your couch. There are 8 different colors that you can choose from. How many different pairs of colors are possible?

20. You and 9 friends are waiting in line at a movie theater. You want to determine how many different orders you and your friends can stand in line. How many different arrangements are possible?

21. A crew boat has 8 different people rowing the boat. There are 12 members on the team. How many different teams of 8 rowers are possible?

22. There are 14 basketball players needing rides. There is room for only 4 basketball players in the coach's car. How many different groups of 4 basketball players are possible?

LESSON 12.7 Practice

For use with pages 632–636

You are given the probability that an event will occur. Find the probability that the event will not occur.

1. $P(A) = 73\%$ **2.** $P(A) = \dfrac{3}{5}$ **3.** $P(A) = 0.41$ **4.** $P(A) = \dfrac{12}{13}$

In Exercises 5–7, you randomly draw a letter tile from a bag. The 11 letters in the word MATHEMATICS are in the bag. Find the probability of choosing the letter described from the bag. Then find the odds in favor of the event.

5. You choose an H. **6.** You choose an A. **7.** You choose an O.

8. An injured football player is told that he has a 40% chance of returning to play next week. What are the odds in favor of the player playing next week?

In Exercises 9–12, find the odds in favor of the event described when rolling a number cube.

9. Roll a 4 or a 5. **10.** Roll a 6 or an 8.

11. Roll a number less than 1. **12.** Roll a number greater than 1.

13. A quarterback completes 24 out of 37 passes. Based on this information, what are the odds that he will complete the next pass he throws?

12.7 Practice

Continued

For use with pages 632–636

In Exercises 14–17, use the spinner to find the probability of the event described.

14. Spin a letter.

15. Spin an even number.

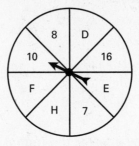

16. Spin a number greater than 7.

17. Spin a vowel.

In Exercises 18–20, use the circle graph that shows the number of people who purchased a T-shirt and the size that they purchased.

18. What is the probability that a randomly chosen person purchasing a T-shirt will buy a medium T-shirt?

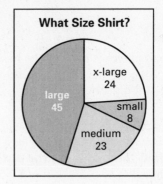

What Size Shirt?

19. What are the odds that a randomly chosen person who purchases a T-shirt will purchase an extra large T-shirt?

20. What are the odds that a randomly chosen person who buys a T-shirt does not purchase a small T-shirt?

Name _____ Date _____

Practice

For use with pages 637–643

Events A and B are independent. Find the missing probability.

1. $P(A) = 0.5$
$P(B) = 0.6$
$P(A \text{ and } B) = $ _____

2. $P(A) = 0.3$
$P(B) = $ _____
$P(A \text{ and } B) = 0.27$

3. $P(A) = $ _____
$P(B) = 0.06$
$P(A \text{ and } B) = 0.03$

Events A and B are dependent. Find the missing probability.

4. $P(A) = 0.31$
$P(B \text{ given } A) = 0.8$
$P(A \text{ and } B) = $ _____

5. $P(A) = 0.7$
$P(B \text{ given } A) = $ _____
$P(A \text{ and } B) = 0.7$

6. $P(A) = $ _____
$P(B \text{ given } A) = 0.6$
$P(A \text{ and } B) = 0.27$

In Exercises 7–9, tell whether the events are *independent* or *dependent*. Then find the probability.

7. You roll a number cube and get a 5. Then you roll the number cube a second time and get a 5 again.

8. A container has 7 green buttons, 3 yellow buttons, and 4 blue buttons. You reach in and randomly draw out a blue button. Then you reach in again and randomly draw out a second blue button.

9. You spin a penny and a nickel on a table. The penny lands heads up and the nickel lands tails up.

Name _____ Date _____

Practice
For use with pages 637–643

10. You are playing a matching game. The game starts with 28 cards face down on a table. There are 14 pairs of cards that match. You start the game by randomly turning over one card, then another to see if they match. What is the probability that you get a match on this first turn?

11. What is the probability that you toss a coin 5 times and get 5 tails in a row? If you have already gotten tails 3 times in a row, what is the probability that you will get tails on the next 2 tosses?

12. At a school bazaar, the principal is going to randomly draw one name from the names of 100 students who entered the drawing. The winner gets tickets to an amusement park. The principal plans to do this 3 days in a row. If the winner's name is replaced, what is the probability of one person winning all 3 days?

Name _____ Date _____

Practice

For use with pages 657–660

Classify the polynomial as a *monomial*, a *binomial*, a *trinomial*, or a *polynomial*.

1. $5x^7 - 8x^3 + x$ **2.** $x - 7y + 1 - x^2$ **3.** $3x^5 + x^7$ **4.** xy^2z

Write the polynomial in standard form.

5. $9 - m + 3m^2$ **6.** $8w + 13 - 9w^4$ **7.** $5b^5 - 4b^3 + 8 - 2b$

Simplify the polynomial and write it in standard form.

8. $9x + 2 - 7x + 12$ **9.** $4x^2 + 5x^3 - 2x^2 + x$

10. $3m^3 + 7m - 2m^2 - m^3$ **11.** $11 - 5d + 6d^2 - 13d$

12. $8c - 9c + 3c^5 + 5c^7 + 3c^5 - 2c$ **13.** $w^6 + 17 - w^4 + 3w^6 - 2w^4$

Write a polynomial expression for the perimeter. Simplify the polynomial.

14.

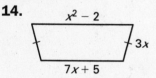

15.

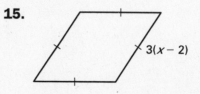

Name _____ Date _____

Practice
For use with pages 657–660

Simplify the polynomial and write it in standard form.

16. $5c^2 - 3 + c - 4c^3 + 8c$

17. $15 + 5m - 3m^2 - 7m + 9m^3 + 8m^2$

18. $6\left(w^3 - 3w^2 + 9w^2 - 4w^3\right)$

19. $-3(2x + 7x^2 + 1) - 3x^2 + 2x - 5x$

In Exercises 20–23, use the following information. David throws a ball off of the observation deck of the Empire State Building that is at a height of 1050 feet. The ball goes up first with a speed of 35 miles per hour or 51 feet per second. Evaluate the polynomial $-16t^2 + 51t + 1050$ to find the height, in feet, after t seconds.

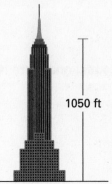

1050 ft

20. 2 sec

21. 3 sec

22. 6 sec

23. 9.5 sec

Simplify the polynomial and write it in standard form.

24. $-3(x + 4x^2 - 3x) + 7x^2 - 2x$

25. $-9(4 + x^2 - 3x + 5) - 2x + 5x^2$

Name _____ Date _____

Practice

For use with pages 661–665

Find the sum.

1. $(x + 3) + (8 - 5x)$

2. $(-4x - 7) + (2x + 9)$

3. $(3x + 10) + (6x - 15)$

4. $(x^2 + 5x) + (9x^2 + 4x)$

5. $(-5x^2 + 8x + 12) + (3x^2 - 4x - 8)$

6. $(6x^2 - 11x - 17) + (9x^2 - 12)$

Find the difference.

7. $(7x - 4) - (x + 3)$

8. $(-6x + 5) - (8x - 2)$

9. $(3x^2 + 10x) - (6x^2 - x)$

10. $(5x^2 + 12x - 17) - (13 - 4x^2 + 8x)$

11. $(9x^2 + 5x + 7) - (4x^2 - 3x + 8)$

12. $(-11x^2 - 12x + 13) - (4x^3 + x^2 - 6)$

Name _____ Date _____

Practice

For use with pages 661-665

Write a polynomial expression for the perimeter of the figure. Simplify the polynomial.

13.

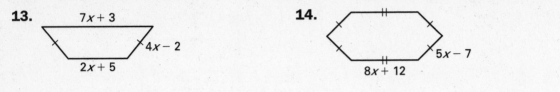

$7x + 3$

$4x - 2$

$2x + 5$

14.

$5x - 7$

$8x + 12$

In Exercises 15–18, simplify the expression.

15. $(7c^3 - 2c + 6) - (12c^2 + 6)$

16. $(5k^2 + 10k - 12) + (-13k^3 + 9k - 16)$

17. $(4w - 7) + (5w + 8) - (w - 3)$

18. $(-6d + 5) - (9d - 8) + d$

19. Find the area of a square that has side length $5x$. If a piece in the center that has an area of $12x^2 - 2$ were cut out of the square, what would be the remaining area of the square?

Perform the indicated operations.

20. $-3(x + 2) - 5(x - 4)$

21. $7(x^2 - 2x + 3) + (4x^2 + 6x - 8)$

22. $6(x^2 - x) + 3(9x^2 - 2x)$

23. $9(x^3 - x^2 + x) - 2(4x^2 - 2x + 7)$

Lesson 13.2

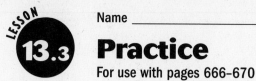

Name _____ Date _____

Practice

For use with pages 666–670

Simplify the expression by multiplying the monomials.

1. $(-5x)(3x^4)$ **2.** $(8x^7)(9x)$ **3.** $(-3x^5)(-2x)$

4. $(12b)(-5b^9)$ **5.** $(-w^8)(-w^3)$ **6.** $(-q^{11})(q^6)$

Simplify the expression by using the distributive property.

7. $t(t - 7)$ **8.** $7m(m + 3)$ **9.** $-k(k^2 - 6)$

10. $-9x(x^5 - x)$ **11.** $a^2(-4a + 15)$ **12.** $12p(8 - p^3)$

Simplify the expression by using the power of a product property.

13. $(4x)^3$ **14.** $(abc)^4$ **15.** $(2xy)^5$ **16.** $(-3q)^2$

17. $(-cd)^7$ **18.** $(5mn)^3$ **19.** $(-6rs)^6$ **20.** $(9ef)^4$

Name _____ Date _____

Practice

For use with pages 666–670

Simplify the expression by using the power of a power property.

21. $\left(x^3\right)^5$ **22.** $\left(a^4\right)^6$ **23.** $\left(b^7\right)^2$ **24.** $\left(e^5\right)^9$

25. $\left(bg^3\right)^4$ **26.** $\left(k^2 l^5\right)^6$ **27.** $\left(3p^4\right)^2$ **28.** $\left(4u^7\right)^3$

Simplify the expression.

29. $3\left(4ab^5\right)^3$ **30.** $-5x^7\left(x^5yz^3\right)^2$ **31.** $\left(-6m^4\right)\left(m^3n^3p\right)$

In Exercises 32–34, simplify and write the expression in scientific notation.

32. $\left(7 \times 10^3\right)^8$ **33.** $\left(3 \times 10^9\right)^4$ **34.** $\left(8 \times 10^8\right)^5$

In Exercises 35–37, use the following information. The surface area of a sphere can be found by using the equation $S = 4\pi r^2$, where S is the surface area and r is the radius. The radius of Earth is approximately 6.38×10^6 meters. The radius of Jupiter is about 7.15×10^7 meters. Determine how many times larger the surface area of Jupiter is than the surface area of Earth. Use 3.14 for π.

35. Determine the surface area of Earth.

36. Determine the surface area of Jupiter.

37. Write a ratio comparing the surface area of Earth to the surface area of Jupiter. Use this ratio to estimate how many times larger Jupiter is than Earth. Round your answer to the nearest whole number.

Lesson 13.3

Name _____ Date _____

Practice

For use with pages 673–677

Match the polynomial to the correct product.

1. $(x + 2)(x + 6)$ **2.** $(x - 3)(x - 4)$ **3.** $(x + 3)(x - 4)$ **4.** $(x + 2)(x - 6)$

A. $x^2 - 7x + 12$ **B.** $x^2 - 4x - 12$ **C.** $x^2 + 8x + 12$ **D.** $x^2 - x - 12$

Find the product and simplify.

5. $(x + 3)(x - 7)$ **6.** $(x + 4)(x + 9)$ **7.** $(x - 12)(x - 6)$

8. $(2m + 3)(m - 4)$ **9.** $(a - 6)(5a - 8)$ **10.** $(-p - 3)(9p - 13)$

11. $(7f - 8)(f - 4)$ **12.** $(5w + 3)(9w - 11)$ **13.** $(4b - 7)(6b + 3)$

14. $\left(\frac{1}{3}x + 4\right)(3x - 9)$ **15.** $\left(\frac{1}{5}x - 2\right)(5x + 15)$ **16.** $(x^2 - 7)(x^2 - 4)$

Practice
For use with pages 673–677

In Exercises 17 and 18, find the polynomial expression for the area of the figure. Simplify the polynomial.

17.

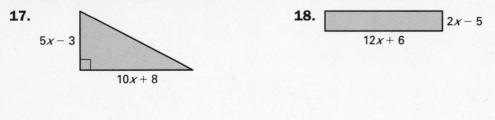

$5x - 3$

$10x + 8$

18.

$12x + 6$

$2x - 5$

19. Explain why $(x - 4)^2$ does not equal $x^2 + 16$.

20. Work backwards to find the unknown binomial in the equation
$x^2 - 4x - 12 = ($_____$)(x - 6)$.

21. You put $25 in a savings account with compound interest. The expression $25(1 + r)^3$, where r is the interest rate, gives the account balance after 3 years. Expand and simplify this expression. Find the account balance if $r = 0.06$.

Name _____ Date _____

Practice

For use with pages 678–685

Rewrite using function notation.

1. $y = 5x^2$

2. $y = -3x^2 - 6$

3. $y = -7x^2$

In Exercises 4–6, evaluate the function using $x = -2$, 0, and 2.

4. $f(x) = 7x^2$

5. $f(x) = 2x^2 - 6$

6. $f(x) = -4x^2$

7. From 1980 to 2000, the cost of tuition C, in dollars, for 1 year at a college can be approximated by the model $C = 8.5x^2 + 4150$, where t is the number of years since 1980. Write this in function notation and find how many years until the tuition is $5000.

Graph the function using a table of values with $x = -3, -2, -1, 0, 1, 2$, and 3.

8. $f(x) = 6x^2$

9. $f(x) = x^2 + 4$

10. $f(x) = -x^2 - 2$

11. $f(x) = -8x^2$

12. $f(x) = 4x^2 + 1$

13. $f(x) = -2x^2 - 4$

Tell whether the graph represents a function.

14.

15.

16.

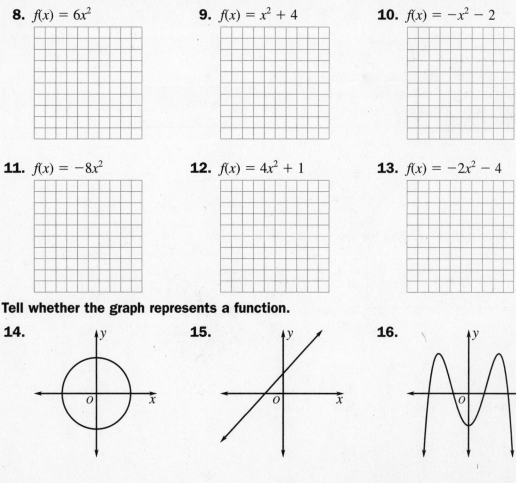

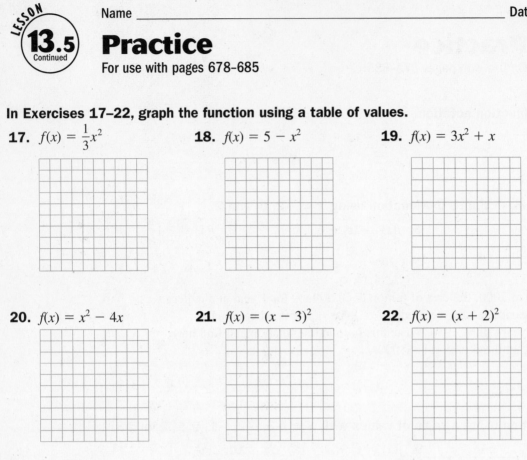

LESSON
13.5
Continued

Name _____ Date _____

Practice
For use with pages 678–685

In Exercises 17–22, graph the function using a table of values.

17. $f(x) = \frac{1}{3}x^2$

18. $f(x) = 5 - x^2$

19. $f(x) = 3x^2 + x$

20. $f(x) = x^2 - 4x$

21. $f(x) = (x - 3)^2$

22. $f(x) = (x + 2)^2$

23. Write a function for the area of the trapezoid using function notation. Graph the function using a table of values. Estimate the value of x if the area of the trapezoid is 42 square meters.

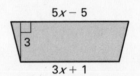

5x − 5

3

3x + 1

Write a function in function notation for the values in the table.

24.

x	−3	−1	0	1	3
$f(x)$	27	3	0	3	27

25.

x	−2	−1	0	1	2
$f(x)$	8	5	4	5	8

Answers

Lesson 1.1

1. bar graph **2.** expensive private college; public college **3.** $100,000

4.

20–24	JHI	5
25–29	III	3
30–34	JHI	5
35–39	IIII	4
40–44	JHI I	6
45–49	JHI JHI	10
50–54	II	2
55–59	I	1

5.

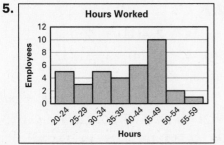

6. histogram **7.** 11 **8.** 0–5.9 and 11–15.9

9. less than 16 pounds **10.** no, a histogram is used when there are equally-spaced intervals for data.

Lesson 1.2

1. multiply: $3 \cdot 3$; 3 **2.** divide: $4 \div 2$; 7

3. subtract: $11 - 3$; 2 **4.** subtract: $9 - 7$; 20

5. add: $5 + 3$; 4 **6.** multiply: 7×8; 63 **7.** 28

8. 6 **9.** 20 **10.** 5 **11.** 10 **12.** 6 **13.** 41 **14.** 60

15. 7 **16.** $89 **17.** 4 **18.** 5 **19.** 20 **20.** 33.6

21. 14.4 **22.** 8.4 **23.** 16.8 **24.** 1.6 **25.** 9

26. $260 **27.** 21 points **28.** 27.5 yds

29. $(7 + 3) \times 4 - 1 = 39$

30. $3 \times (6 - 1) + 2 = 17$

31. $(9 - 4 + 2) \times 7 = 49$

32. $(6 - 3) \times (7 + 4) = 33$

Lesson 1.3

1. addition **2.** division **3.** multiplication

4. multiplication **5.** subtraction **6.** addition

7. division **8.** subtraction **9.** 22 **10.** 17

11. 18 **12.** 9 **13.** 40 **14.** 16 **15.** 0 **16.** 102

17. $8 + x$ **18.** $x \div 3$ **19.** $x - 14$ **20.** $9x$

21. $2.4n + 112n + 26.2n$; 562.4 mi

22. $3p + 4b$; $41 **23.** 4.8 **24.** 21.6 **25.** 8 **26.** 54

27. 1.6 **28.** 16.22 **29.** $21g - 107$; 19 miles

Lesson 1.4

1. C **2.** B **3.** A **4.** 125 **5.** 81 **6.** 256 **7.** 343

8. 121 **9.** 0 **10.** 4^5; four to the fifth power

11. 12^2; twelve squared **12.** w^3; w cubed **13.** 8

14. 10 **15.** 271 **16.** 89 **17.** 4 **18.** 21 **19.** 49

20. 130 **21.** 91 **22.** 64 **23.** 96 ft **24.** < **25.** >

26. = **27.** 59.36 **28.** 405.16 **29.** 74.088

30. s^2; 49 in.^{2}

Lesson 1.5

1. B **2.** D **3.** A **4.** C **5.** 7 **6.** 16 **7.** 20 **8.** 5

9. 7 **10.** 11 **11.** 12 **12.** 7 **13.** 225 **14.** yes

15. yes **16.** no **17.** no **18.** $120 = 6x$; $20

19. $35 = 17 + x$; 18 pages **20.** substitute 7 for x and evaluate 56/7 to see if it equals 8.

21. Multiply 20 by 60 (1 min = 60 sec) by adding two zeros to the product 2×6: 1200 sec

22. $6000 = 3x$; 2000 miles each month

23. $39 = 16 + x$; $23

Lesson 1.6

1. $P = 34$ in.; $A = 30$ in.^{2} **2.** $P = 24$ cm; $A = 36$ cm^2 **3.** $P = 26$ ft; $A = 36$ ft^2

4. $P = 22$ mm; $A = 28$ mm^2 **5.** $P = 16$ km; $A = 12$ km^2 **6.** $P = 32$ in.; $A = 55$ in.^{2}

7. $P = 42$ yd; $A = 104$ yd^2 **8.** 9 in. **9.** 3 yd

10. 5 km **11.** 3 min **12.** 12 in./sec **13.** 330 ft

14. 93.5 cm **15.** about 5.8 sec **16.** 189 mi

17. 1050 ft^2; 130 ft; 55 ft; 150 ft

18. about 0.94 hours or 56.7 minutes

Lesson 1.7

1. 16 hours **2.** $230 **3.** $3.59 **4.** 8 oz canned tomatoes, 1 cup cooked macaroni **5.** 27; 34

6. 3; 1 **7.** 7; 4 **8.** 512; 4096 **9.** 4 and 9

10. 2420 **11.** 1060 **12.** $81x$; $243x$ **13.** $22x^2$; $28x^2$

14. $31x$; $9x$ **15.** $31x^5$; $34x^6$

Lesson 2.1

1. negative **2.** positive **3.** $-24, -16, -8, 2, 7,$

Lesson 2.1 *continued*

17, 23 **4.** −136, −56, −38, −24, −16, 11, 25, 102 **5.** −10, −7, −5, −1, 0, 2, 4, 6 **6.** −84, −51, −39, −15, 8, 17, 73 **7.** −7; 7 **8.** 25; 25

9. −106; 106 **10.** 241; 241 **11.** < **12.** >

13. < **14.** < **15.** > **16.** > **17.** E **18.** D

19. C **20.** A **21.** B **22.** 15 **23.** 9 **24.** −16

25. −6 **26.** 49 **27.** −34 **28.** Juanita **29.** Sarah

30. Juanita, Beth, Tamika, Sarah, Ingrid

Lesson 2.2

1. −4 + 11; 7 **2.** 1 **3.** −5 **4.** −9 **5.** 9

6. −17 **7.** −97 **8.** −7 **9.** 9 **10.** −41

11. −43 **12.** −68 **13.** −121 **14.** never

15. never **16.** never **17.** sometimes **18.** −13

19. −9 **20.** −30 **21.** −140 **22.** $227 **23.** 2

Lesson 2.3

1. −4 **2.** −15 **3.** 7 **4.** −21 **5.** −5 **6.** −3

7. 40 **8.** −14 **9.** −16 **10.** −11 **11.** −12

12. −95 **13.** −6 − 19; −25 **14.** 8 − (−21); 29

15. −15 − (−28); 13 **16.** 10 **17.** −28 **18.** −29

19. $483 **20.** 47 ft **21.** −247 **22.** −75 **23.** 846

24. 3 **25.** −12 **26.** −24 **27.** −1 **28.** −8

29. −88 **30.** −31 **31.** 15 **32.** 9 **33.** −10

34. −12 **35.** −9 **36.** d **37.** It went down 67 cents.

Lesson 2.4

1. −36 **2.** 35 **3.** 0 **4.** 99 **5.** −96 **6.** 260

7. −306 **8.** 288 **9.** −210 **10.** 792 **11.** 0

12. −455 **13.** 126 **14.** −462 **15.** 113 **16.** 30

17. −4851 **18.** −378 **19.** 48 **20.** −63 **21.** 160

22. −7 **23.** 3 **24.** −5 **25.** 15 **26.** the 17-yard line **27.** −78 **28.** −6084 **29.** 8281 **30.** 23 steps behind the original position **31.** $132

Lesson 2.5

1. 8 **2.** −8 **3.** −5 **4.** 0 **5.** undefined **6.** −12

7. −2 **8.** −8 **9.** −9 **10.** 8 **11.** −21 **12.** 5

13. 4 **14.** −3 **15.** −2 **16.** −48 **17.** −6

18. 6 **19.** 4 **20.** −5 **21.** −6 **22.** 3 **23.** −6

24. Woods: 276; Goosen: 279; Mickelson: 280; Olazabal: 281; Harrington, Els: 282; Singh: 283, Garcia: 284; Jimenez, Scott, Cabrera: 285

25. 282 **26.** 282; The numbers are the same.

Lesson 2.6

1. *b; a* **2.** *b; a* **3.** *a; b; c* **4.** *a; b; c*

5. 5; Associative of Addition **6.** 12; Commutative of Multiplication **7.** 5; Associative of Multiplication **8.** 51; Commutative of Addition

9. 69 **10.** −52 **11.** −2 **12.** 21 **13.** −65

14. 13,000 **15.** −130 **16.** 900 **17.** 88

18. −90*x* **19.** *x* − 64 **20.** *x* + 93 **21.** *x* − 47

22. *x* + 3 **23.** 357*x* **24.** 4 **25.** 36 miles north

26. 5.5 **27.** 720 **28.** 81 **29.** $2\frac{2}{5}$ **30.** −65 **31.** 66

Lesson 2.7

1. −5*y* + (−5)(7) **2.** 4(11) + 4(6)

3. 6(8) + 6*m* **4.** −31(24) + (−31)(12)

5. 13(7) + 13*w* + 13(−9)

6. −29*p* − (−29)(21) − (−29)(5) **7.** 9*c* + 5*d*

8. 10*m* + 12*k* **9.** 13*s* + 4*t* **10.** 12*c* + 5*d*

11. −20*g* − 16*h* **12.** 19*x* + 3*y* **13.** 224 in.²

14. 297 mm² **15.** 12*w* − 96 **16.** −33*x*

17. 7*x* − 8 **18.** 26*d* **19.** 10*p* **20.** 4*g* − 32

21. Multiply the total cost of a necklace and earrings, $30, by 7. The total cost is $210.

22. $83.58 **23.** 105 **24.** 92 **25.** 216

26. 1560 **27.** 15(27 + 31); 870 ft²

Lesson 2.8

1. (6, −2) **2.** (0, −3) **3.** (−3, 1) **4.** (1, 5)

5. (4, 0) **6.** (3, −7)

Graph for 7–12.

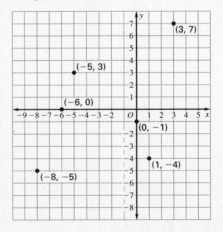

7. left 5, up 3 from origin, Quadrant II

Lesson 2.8 *continued*

8. right 1, down 4 from origin, Quadrant IV

9. down 1 from origin, *y*-axis **10.** right 3, up 7 from origin, Quadrant I **11.** left 6 from origin, *x*-axis **12.** left 8, down 5 from origin, Quadrant III

13. rectangle; 14

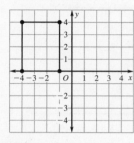

14. rectangle; 26

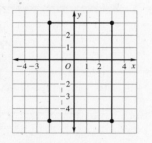

15. square; 20

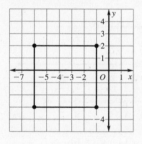

16. The points lie on a line.

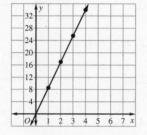

17. $51

18. $P = 26$ units; $A = 40$ square units

19. $P = 26$ units; $A = 42$ square units

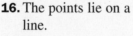
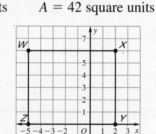

20. $P = 22$ units; $A = 30$ square units

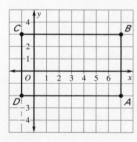
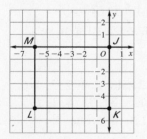

Lesson 3.1

1. 2 **2.** 23 **3.** −7 **4.** 31 **5.** 68 **6.** 17 **7.** −12

8. 17 **9.** 20 **10.** 52 **11.** 51 **12.** 6 **13.** yes

14. no; $c + 7 = 21.95$ **15.** no; $125 = p - 34$

16. no; $d - 2\frac{1}{2} = 2\frac{1}{4}$ **17.** Answers may vary.

18. 0 **19.** $\frac{10}{8}$ **20.** 3.4 **21.** 3.24 **22.** $\frac{2}{5}$ **23.** 4.037

24. Total Miles = Miles Already Driven + Miles Left to Drive; $275 = 132 + m$; 143 miles

Lesson 3.2

1. 7; 7; 5 **2.** 2; 2; −48 **3.** 64 **4.** 56 **5.** 30 **6.** 8

7. 6 **8.** 7 **9.** 96 **10.** 260 **11.** 374 **12.** 15

13. 4 **14.** 8 **15.** B **16.** Divide by 9. **17.** Multiply by −6. **18.** Subtract −11. **19.** −36 **20.** −13

21. 17 **22.** 15.2 **23.** −26.13 **24.** 60 **25.** −15

26. −44.1 **27.** 90 **28.** 4 **29.** −116.1 **30.** −20

31. $160

Lesson 3.3

1. 4 **2.** 7 **3.** 3 **4.** 9 **5.** −10 **6.** −2 **7.** 18

8. −3 **9.** 9 **10.** 11 **11.** 8 **12.** 14

13. 8(2) + 1; 17 pints **4.** $2.34 **15.** $-\frac{1}{2}$ **16.** 64

17. 24 **18.** 72 **19.** 72 **20.** −7 **21.** 3 **22.** 6

23. 486 **24.** −833 **25.** 6 **26.** 256 **27.** 8 lawns

28. 7 tickets **29.** 1 **30.** −20 **31.** 2

Lesson 3.4

1. B **2.** $8 - \frac{n}{6} = 9$; $n = -6$

3. $4n + 10 = 22$; $n = 3$ **4.** 3 hours

5. 14,800 miles **6.** Answers may vary.

7. 5 packages **8.** $7n + 3 = 59$; $n = 8$

9. $4n - \frac{2}{3} = \frac{34}{3}$; $n = 3$ **10.** $24 - \frac{n}{6} = -5$;

$n = 174$ **11.** $9.8 + \frac{n}{5} = 10.4$; $n = 3$

12. $4\left(\frac{n}{7}\right) = 24$; $n = 42$ **13.** $8n - \left(\frac{-54}{9}\right) = -18$;

$n = -3$ **14.** $\left(\frac{6^2}{4}\right)n = 117$; $n = 13$

Lesson 3.5

1. 18 m²; 25 m **2.** 16.5 in.²; 34.5 in.

3. 24 yd²; 24 yd **4.** 12 yd **5.** 3 m **6.** 8 cm

7. 4 mm **8.** 7 in. **9.** 14 yd **10.** 13 mm

11. 48 in. **12.** $\frac{37}{4.2x}$ ft **13.** $\frac{39}{8.1w}$ cm **14.** 135 in.²

15. 104 ft²

Lesson 3.6

1. B **2.** D **3.** C **4.** A **5.** f is greater than or equal to -4. **6.** d is less than 9. **7.** w is greater than -19. **8.** g is less than or equal to 0.

9. $x > 1$

10. $13 \geq m$

11. $p < -2$

12. $8 > f$

13. $16 \leq a$

14. $y > -2$

15. $q \geq -13$

16. $v \leq -22$

17. $-3 > j$

18. $4.2 < k$

19. $m > 3\frac{2}{3}$

20. $t < 10.5$

21. no **22.** yes **23.** yes **24.** yes

25. $x + 26 < 30; x < 4$

26.

27. x is less than 4 and greater than -3.

28. 8 is less than or equal to h, which is less than or equal to 13.

29. w is greater than 0 and less than or equal to 7.

Lesson 3.7

1. $m > 12$

2. $h \leq -72$

3. $y \geq -145$

4. $p < -51$

5. $g < 6$

6. $-4 \leq n$

7. $k < -11$

8. $q \geq -8$

9. $-108 < u$

10. $c \leq -8$

11. $b > -427$

12. $4 \geq j$

13. $6m \geq 438; m \geq 73$ **14.** at least 44 hours

15. $x > -6$

16. $y > -17$

17. $p \geq 7$

18. $-13 \geq m$

19. $d < -15$

20. $z \leq -5$

21. at most 44 stamps **22.** $x \geq 18$ **23.** $x \leq 2$

24. $x \leq -8$ **25.** 7, 8, 9 **26.** at least 116 tickets

Lesson 4.1

1. 1, 2, 3, 4, 6, 8, 12, 16, 24, 48 **2.** 1, 2, 3, 4, 6, 8, 9, 12, 18, 24, 36, 72 **3.** 1, 3, 31, 93 **4.** 1, 2, 3, 6, 7, 9, 14, 18, 21, 42, 63, 126 **5.** prime

6. composite **7.** composite **8.** prime **9.** 2^4

10. $5 \cdot 7$ **11.** $2 \cdot 5^2$ **12.** $2^4 \cdot 3^2$ **13.** 34; 17; 2; 2; 2 **14.** 18; 5; 9; 5; 3; 3; 2 **15.** 10; 4; 5; 2; 4; 2; 5; 2; 2; 2; 2; 2; 2; 5 **16.** $2 \cdot 2 \cdot 2 \cdot a \cdot a \cdot b$

17. $2 \cdot 3 \cdot 5 \cdot x \cdot x \cdot y \cdot y$

Lesson 4.1 *continued*

18. $3 \cdot 3 \cdot 5 \cdot m \cdot m \cdot m \cdot n \cdot n$

19. $2 \cdot 2 \cdot 3 \cdot 7 \cdot b \cdot b \cdot c \cdot c \cdot c \cdot d$ **20.** 1, 5, 25, 125 **21.** 1, 7, 49, 343 **22.** 1, 3, 7, 9, 11, 21, 33, 63, 77, 99, 231, 693 **23.** 1, 2, 4, 5, 10, 20, 25, 50, 100, 125, 250, 500 **24.** 1 room with 162 students, 2 with 81, 3 with 54, 6 with 27; 6 rooms with 27 students; Answers may vary.

25. Sample Answer:

```
   124              124
   / \              / \
  4 × 31          2 × 62
 / \  / \        / \  / \
2 × 2 × 31    2 × 2 × 32; yes
```

26. $2^3 \cdot 3^2 \cdot 5$ **27.** $2 \cdot 7^3$ **28.** $2^6 \cdot 3^3$
29. $2^4 \cdot 3^2 \cdot 13$

Lesson 4.2

1. B **2.** A **3.** D **4.** C **5.** 2 **6.** 8 **7.** 7 **8.** no; 3
9. no; 9 **10.** no; 13 **11.** yes **12.** yes **13.** no; 5
14. no; 16 **15.** no; 23 **16.** no; 28
17. $36 = 2^2 \cdot 3^2$, $52 = 2^2 \cdot 13$, $48 = 2^4 \cdot 3$, $24 = 2^3 \cdot 3$ **18.** 2^2 **19.** 4; 4 plates can be made.
20. $9x^2$ **21.** $14xy$ **22.** $4xy^2$ **23.** y **24.** 18
25. $13xyz$ **26.** The first number; the first number is a factor of the second **27.** 4 hours; Cheryl–8 shifts, Mark–9 shifts, Jeremy–3 shifts, Tonya–4 shifts **28.** *Sample Answer*: 8, 16

Lesson 4.3

1. $\frac{6}{7}$ **2.** $\frac{2}{3}$ **3.** $\frac{17}{18}$ **4.** $\frac{2}{3}$ **5.** $-\frac{2}{5}$ **6.** $-\frac{3}{7}$ **7.** $\frac{13b}{15}$
8. $-\frac{3}{11y}$ **9.** yes **10.** no **11.** no **12.** yes
13–16. Answers may vary. **17.** 28 **18.** $\frac{432}{343}$
19. $-\frac{2}{3}$ **20.** $\frac{16,807}{2304}$ **21.** -702 **22.** $\frac{23}{117}$ **23.** $\frac{32}{117}$
24. $\frac{56}{117}$ **25.** $\frac{6}{7}, \frac{6}{7}$; yes **26.** $\frac{99}{100}, \frac{9}{10}$; no
27. $\frac{28}{51}, \frac{28}{51}$; yes **28.** $\frac{12}{13}, \frac{154}{169}$; no **29.** $\frac{16}{17}, \frac{16}{17}$; yes
30. $\frac{26}{31}, \frac{26}{31}$; yes

Lesson 4.4

1. B **2.** D **3.** A **4.** C **5.** 30 **6.** 48 **7.** 45
8. 140 **9.** $12 = 2^2 \cdot 3$, $72 = 2^3 \cdot 3^2$; LCM = 72
10. $28 = 2^2 \cdot 7$, $42 = 2 \cdot 3 \cdot 7$; LCM = 84

11. $36 = 2^2 \cdot 3^2$, $39 = 3 \cdot 13$; LCM = 468
12. $20 = 2^2 \cdot 5$, $70 = 2 \cdot 5 \cdot 7$; LCM = 140
13. $6 = 2 \cdot 3$, $9 = 3^2$, $12 = 2^2 \cdot 3$; LCM = 36
14. $20 = 2^2 \cdot 5$, $24 = 2^3 \cdot 3$, $28 = 2^2 \cdot 7$; LCM = 840 **15.** $14 = 2 \cdot 7$, $21 = 3 \cdot 7$, $30 = 3 \cdot 2 \cdot 5$; LCM = 210 **16.** $40 = 2^3 \cdot 5$, $60 = 2^2 \cdot 3 \cdot 5$, $24 = 2^3 \cdot 3$; LCM = 120
17. $48 = 2^4 \cdot 3$, $56 = 2^3 \cdot 7$, $64 = 2^6$; LCM = 1344 **18.** $36a^2b^2$ **19.** $25c^4d^4$ **20.** $84p^3q^4$
21. 336 days **22.** 42 days; Sunday **23.** 670
24. 2904 **25.** 2184 **26.** 1638 **27.** 480 **28.** 8610
29. $45x^2y^3$ **30.** $44a^4b^7$ **31.** $84p^4q^4$ **32.** 60 shots

Lesson 4.5

1. 24 **2.** 18 **3.** 60 **4.** 210 **5.** = **6.** > **7.** <
8. < **9.** > **10.** = **11.** < **12.** > **13.** >
14. $\frac{1}{12}, \frac{1}{4}, \frac{9}{16}, \frac{5}{8}$ **15.** $\frac{5}{6}, \frac{13}{9}, 1\frac{15}{18}$
16. $\frac{81}{24}, \frac{28}{8}, \frac{65}{18}, 4\frac{2}{3}$ **17.** $\frac{11}{13}, \frac{11}{12}, \frac{7}{3}, \frac{5}{2}$
18. $\frac{27}{20}, \frac{21}{15}, 2\frac{4}{5}, 2\frac{10}{12}$ **19.** $2\frac{1}{12}, \frac{19}{9}, \frac{34}{15}, \frac{41}{18}$
20. Shawnda **21.** $\frac{23}{50}, \frac{15}{27}$; Todd **22.** the second
review **23.** < **24.** = **25.** >

Lesson 4.6

1. yes **2.** no **3.** no **4.** yes **5.** 6^{12} **6.** 12^4 **7.** x^{12}
8. a^8 **9.** w^5 **10.** 13^7 **11.** 9 **12.** m^6 **13.** b^{17}
14. k^7 **15.** $(-5)^9$ **16.** $(-15)^4$ **17.** should be $2 + 5$ for the exponent in the first line **18.** 7
19. 3 **20.** 1 **21.** 13 **22.** 4^2p^8 **23.** 11^2f^{11}
24. $6^5a^7b^9$ **25.** u^2v **26.** z^5 **27.** $12r^4$ **28.** $23m^6$
29. $14^5r^{12}s^9$ **30.** $10^4x^{10}y^3$ **31.** $2^3 \cdot 2^3 \cdot 2^3 = 2^9$
32. $4^5 = 1024 \text{ ft}^2$; 512 minutes

Lesson 4.7

1. $\frac{1}{625}$ **2.** $\frac{1}{262,144}$ **3.** $\frac{1}{1024}$ **4.** 1 **5.** $-\frac{1}{81}$ **6.** 11
7. 1 **8.** $\frac{1}{49}$ **9.** g^3 **10.** 1 **11.** $\frac{7}{p^6}$ **12.** $\frac{1}{j^{16}}$ **13.** $\frac{1}{b^7}$
14. $\frac{6}{x^9}$ **15.** $\frac{1}{c^{14}}$ **16.** $\frac{3}{d^{11}}$ **17.** $\frac{13}{z^{30}}$ **18.** $\frac{w^4}{7^9}$
19. $\frac{s^{11}}{14^{11}t^4}$ **20.** $\frac{a^5}{b^7}$ **21.** 0 **22.** -6 **23.** -13
24. -7 **25.** -13 **26.** 7 **27.** $\frac{\text{kg} \cdot \text{m}}{\text{s}^2}$ **28.** $\frac{\text{kg} \cdot \text{m}^2}{\text{s}^3 \cdot \text{A}}$
29. 1.66×10^{-6} attograms **30.** 5.87 terameters

Lesson 4.8

1. 7.3×10^5 **2.** 6.1×10^3 **3.** 8.915×10^9
4. 7.48×10^{-5} **5.** 9.3×10^{-4} **6.** 5.6×10^{-8}
7. 0.0000804 **8.** 0.000000000000526
9. 0.0139 **10.** 4110 **11.** 761,000,000,000
12. 745,000,000 **13.** 4.2×10^9 **14.** 1.6×10^8
15. 1.598×10^9 **16.** 3.024×10^{17}
17. 216,000,000 **18.** 5.97×10^{24}
19. < **20.** > **21.** > **22.** = **23.** 3.496×10^{-11}
24. 4.002×10^3 **25.** 9.75×10^1 **26.** 3.41×10^{-21}
27. 3.9×10^1 **28.** 8.5×10^5 **29.** 5.3×10^2
30. 1.05 **31.** 1.65

Lesson 5.1

1. $\frac{7}{8} - \frac{3}{8} = \frac{4}{8}$ or $\frac{1}{2}$ **2.** $\frac{7}{8}$ **3.** $-\frac{1}{3}$ **4.** $\frac{1}{2}$ **5.** $3\frac{1}{2}$
6. $-2\frac{2}{5}$ **7.** $\frac{2}{3}$ **8.** $-\frac{2}{3}$ **9.** $-4\frac{1}{2}$ **10.** $3\frac{1}{2}$ **11.** $1\frac{h}{3}$
12. $-\frac{x}{5y}$ **13.** $-\frac{v}{w}$ **14.** $\frac{3}{4}$ pound **15.** $6\frac{5}{6}$ hours
16. $\frac{13}{14}$ **17.** $-\frac{1}{2}$ **18.** $-\frac{1}{3}$ **19.** $-\frac{7}{18}$ **20.** $-6\frac{3}{4}$
21. $2\frac{11}{12}$ **22.** $x = \frac{2}{3}$ **23.** $w = \frac{2}{5}$ **24.** $b = 1\frac{1}{4}$

Lesson 5.2

1. $\frac{5}{8}$ **2.** $\frac{77}{90}$ **3.** $1\frac{37}{65}$ **4.** $-\frac{31}{88}$ **5.** $-\frac{1}{140}$ **6.** $-1\frac{2}{5}$
7. $4\frac{5}{42}$ **8.** $9\frac{5}{21}$ **9.** $4\frac{83}{104}$ **10.** $11\frac{11}{40}$ **11.** $11\frac{107}{120}$
12. $11\frac{13}{24}$ **13.** Stephanie **14.** $5\frac{7}{24}$ pies **15.** false
16. true **17.** false **18.** $-\frac{16x}{45}$ **19.** $-\frac{m}{55}$
20. $\frac{70 + 26p}{91p}$ **21.** $1\frac{79}{168q}$ **22.** $x = 2\frac{1}{2}$ **23.** $y = 3\frac{5}{6}$
24. $w = 2\frac{13}{16}$ **25.** $4\frac{7}{8}$ yards

Lesson 5.3

1. $\frac{1}{20}$ **2.** $\frac{8}{27}$ **3.** $\frac{9}{20}$ **4.** -1 **5.** 12 **6.** $10\frac{1}{2}$
7. $30\frac{13}{45}$ **8.** $-27\frac{1}{7}$ **9.** $29\frac{3}{5}$ **10.** $\frac{7}{18}$ **11.** $\frac{33}{52}$
12. $-\frac{77}{120}$ **13.** $2\frac{13}{32}$ **14.** $1555\frac{1}{2}$ m^2 **15.** $2\frac{4}{25}$ m^2
16. $168\frac{2}{7}$ in.^{2} **17.** $71\frac{91}{99}$ cm^2 **18.** $-\frac{14}{135}$ **19.** -6
20. $7\frac{13}{28}$ **21.** $\frac{91}{225}$

Lesson 5.4

1. $\frac{17}{3}$ **2.** $-\frac{22}{7}$ **3.** $\frac{1}{12}$ **4.** $\frac{10}{39}$ **5.** $\frac{2}{7}$ **6.** $-\frac{4}{15}$ **7.** $\frac{98}{165}$
8. $-1\frac{29}{192}$ **9.** $\frac{3}{26}$ **10.** $-\frac{1}{22}$ **11.** $1\frac{23}{32}$ **12.** $-\frac{329}{402}$
13. $2\frac{1}{102}$ **14.** $-\frac{57}{80}$ **15.** $\frac{51}{98}$ **16.** $-4\frac{103}{119}$
17. $a = 16$ **18.** $b = -30$ **19.** $w = 91$ **20.** 6
21. $10\frac{1}{6}$ pieces **22.** 10 **23.** $\frac{5}{14}$ **24.** -20
25. $98\frac{3}{10}$ yd

Lesson 5.5

1. C **2.** A **3.** B **4.** integer, whole number, rational number **5.** rational number **6.** rational number **7.** integer, rational number **8.** 0.6
9. $-0.\overline{4}$ **10.** $-0.\overline{81}$ **11.** 0.6875 **12.** 3.125
13. $-5.\overline{148}$ **14.** $7.\overline{48}$ **15.** 0.825 **16.** -0.07
17. 0.5 **18.** -8.38 **19.** $-0.\overline{6930}$ **20.** $\frac{6}{25}$
21. $-\frac{61}{100}$ **22.** $2\frac{12}{25}$ **23.** $7\frac{3}{20}$ **24.** $-\frac{1}{3}$ **25.** $\frac{19}{20}$
26. $-\frac{124}{999}$ **27.** $-\frac{109}{1000}$ **28.** $\frac{3}{4}$, 0.8, 0.81, $\frac{11}{13}$, $\frac{6}{7}$
29. $6\frac{2}{19}$, $6\frac{1}{8}$, 6.15, $6\frac{1}{5}$, 6.3 **30.** Warner: $0.\overline{6}$;
Collins: $0.\overline{846153}$; Griese: 0.7; Garcia: 0.75;
Favre: $0.65\overline{90}$ **31.** Collins, Garcia, Griese, Favre, Warner

Lesson 5.6

1. 19.303 **2.** 1.868 **3.** -3.546 **4.** -3.58
5. 3.684 **6.** -19.445 **7.** -9.608 **8.** 43.758
9. 16.569 **10.** -5.85 **11.** 36.307 **12.** -1.075
13. $f = 30.7$ **14.** $g = 7.81$ **15.** $h = 23.01$
16. $j = 17.685$ **17.** $k = -1.444$
18. $m = -15.072$ **19.** 31 **20.** 64 **21.** 98 **22.** 132
23. \$135.25 **24.** 18.38 cm **25.** 34.6 m
26. 31.48 in. **27.** $100 + 70 + 5 + 0.9 + 0.02 + 0.003 + 0.0001$ **28.** 7.125 yd **29.** no
30. 0.075 yd

Lesson 5.7

1. C **2.** B **3.** A **4.** 2.56 **5.** 67.34 **6.** -1.792
7. 9 **8.** 24.5 **9.** -28.15 **10.** -173.3418
11. 3.87 **12.** 14.25 **13.** 0.89 **14.** 0.0114 **15.** 7.4
16. Area = length $\times$ width

Lesson 5.7 *continued*

17. A = 0.305×0.305; 0.093025 km^2
18. $0.3 \times 0.3 = 0.09$ **19.** 6.234375 **20.** 0.9
21. 15.906 **22.** -0.06966 **23.** -25.44
24. 23.6898 **25.** 21.5 patties **26.** 22.75 in.^{2}
27. -2.91 **28.** 4 **29.** 37.73 **30.** \$3.59

Lesson 5.8

1. mean: -25; median: -21; mode: -6;
range: 46 **2.** mean: 67; median:73; no mode;
range: 88 **3.** mean: 174; median: 164.5; no mode;
range: 131 **4.** mean: 65; median: 75; no mode;
range: 68 **5.** mean: 4; median: 4; mode: 4;
range: 5 **6.** mean: 8; median: 7.75; no mode;
range: 3.5 **7.** mean: 32.3; median: 31; no mode;
range: 31 **8.** mean: 204.29; median: 193; no
mode; range: 87; Best average: median, because 4
of the 7 were at or below this number. **9.** \$43.01
10. $2x$

Lesson 6.1

1. no; 2 **2.** yes **3.** yes **4.** no; 13 **5.** 4 **6.** 6
7. -3 **8.** 22 **9.** -6 **10.** 3 **11.** 31 **12.** -15
13. 11 **14.** \$109.10 **15.** \$11.25 **16.** -1.875
17. 0 **18.** -2 **19.** 332 **20.** 43 m **21.** 42 yd

Lesson 6.2

1. 8 **2.** 6 **3.** 4 **4.** -9 **5.** 6 **6.** -8 **7.** 2 **8.** 19
9. -7 **10.** 54 units **11.** 45 units **12.** 122 units
13. 1 **14.** -6 **15.** 3 **16.** 8 **17.** 12 **18.** 11
19. 9 months **20.** When each has read for 6 hours
21. \$3 each; \$153 **22.** 7 **23.** $\frac{1}{5}$ **24.** 5 **25.** -2
26. -21 **27.** -2

Lesson 6.3

1. 100; -2.4 **2.** 100; 3 **3.** 100; 4.15 **4.** 9; $\frac{4}{11}$
5. 20; $\frac{2}{3}$ **6.** 42; $13\frac{1}{29}$ **7.** Third and fourth lines
should be $6 = -6x$ and $x = -1$ **8.** -6.2
9. 8 **10.** 4.3 **11.** $-2\frac{1}{2}$ **12.** $1\frac{5}{39}$ **13.** $1\frac{11}{91}$
14. 3 h 10 min **15.** \$2.15; \$37.65 **16.** 5.8
17. 1.8 **18.** -1 **19.** $\frac{25}{227}$

Lesson 6.4

1. 13.5 m **2.** 28 yd **3.** 32.45 in.; not a multiple
of 7 **4.** 34.54 mm; not a multiple of 7 **5.** 1.5 ft;

multiple of 3.14 **6.** 140 cm; multiple of $\frac{22}{7}$
7. 8.478 cm **8.** 103.62 mm **9.** 3.14 in.
10. 4.7 cm; not a multiple of 7 **11.** 1.9 cm; not a
multiple of 7 **12.** 66 cm; multiple of 7
13. about 4.63 ft; about 29.05 ft **14.** about
20.01 ft **15.** about 21.98 mm

Lesson 6.5

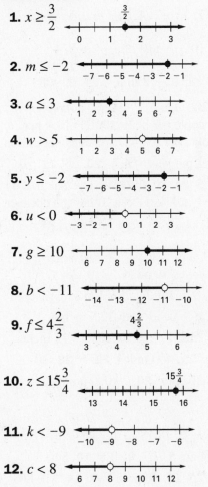

1. $x \geq \frac{3}{2}$

2. $m \leq -2$

3. $a \leq 3$

4. $w > 5$

5. $y \leq -2$

6. $u < 0$

7. $g \geq 10$

8. $b < -11$

9. $f \leq 4\frac{2}{3}$

10. $z \leq 15\frac{3}{4}$

11. $k < -9$

12. $c < 8$

13. $y \geq 112.6$; He needs to get at least 112.6 yards
per game. **14.** $800 \geq 260 + 40x + 50x$; $x \leq 6$; At
most, 6 groups of 40 and 6 groups of 50 people
can fit. **15.** $z \leq 11\frac{1}{9}$ **16.** $h < 126$ **17.** $c \geq -143$
18. $a \geq 3.1$ **19.** $z \leq -96.5$ **20.** $p \leq 9.2$
21. $p \geq \$268.50$; Frank needs to save at least
\$268.50 a month.

Lesson 6.6

1. $x \leq 12$ **2.** $x + 9 < 5$; $x < -4$ **3.** $3x \geq 20$;
$x \geq 6\frac{2}{3}$ **4.** $18 - x \leq 19$; $x \geq -1$ **5.** D **6.** A

Lesson 6.6 continued

7. B **8.** C **9.** $500 \le 6x + 116$; $x \ge 64$;
at least 64 cars **10.** 9 months or less; no
11. $2{,}000{,}000 \le 1{,}250{,}000 + 7x - 762{,}500$;
$x \ge 216{,}071.43$; need to make at least \$216,071.43
a week **12.** less than \$30.40; Answers may vary.

Lesson 7.1

1. $\frac{4}{5}$, 4 to 5, 4 : 5 **2.** $\frac{9}{17}$, 9 to 17, 9 : 17

3. $\frac{3}{-7}$, 3 to -7, 3 : -7 **4.** $\frac{3}{2}$, 3 to 2, 3 : 2

5. $\frac{-3}{10}$, -3 to 10, -3 : 10 **6.** $\frac{4}{5}$, 4 to 5, 4 : 5

7. $\frac{3}{1}$, 3 to 1, 3 : 1 **8.** $\frac{8}{3}$, 8 to 3, 8 : 3 **9.** 900

10. 720 **11.** 1200 **12.** 2.33 **13.** 54 points per
game **14.** 40 people per boat **15.** 62 miles per
hour **16.** 24 hours per day **17.** 32 cups per gallon
18. 0.625 inches per year **19.** 1 **20.** 25 **21.** 20
22. 14 **23.** 4 : 6 **24.** 8 : 4 **25.** Casey; She had a
faster unit speed. **26.** large can; It has the cheaper
unit price.

Lesson 7.2

1. no **2.** yes **3.** yes **4.** no **5.** 32 **6.** 28 **7.** 52
8. 8 **9.** 3 **10.** 0.7 **11.** 3.2 **12.** 1 **13.** 5.13
14. 3 inches **15.** 9 inches **16.** 12.5 inches
17. 17.5 inches **18.** 7.6 inches **19.** 13.75 inches
20. 144 players **21.** 400 miles **22.** 5 **23.** 10
24. 3 **25.** 42 deliveries **26.** 29,000 points

Lesson 7.3

1. 80% **2.** 85% **3.** 18.18% **4.** 7.41% **5.** 12
6. 89.04 **7.** 14.26 **8.** 7.7 **9.** 128 **10.** 840
11. 416 **12.** 1775 **13.** 40 problems **14.** \$10.80
15. 174.4% **16.** 12.8% **17.** 324.48 **18.** 0.288
19. 89.13 **20.** 180,000 **21.** 42 **22.** 62.5%
23. 324 **24.** 49.3% **25.** 12.5% **26.** 15.12y
27. 20y

Lesson 7.4

1. 5% **2.** 2456% **3.** 36.2% **4.** 0.7% **5.** 37.5%
6. 86% **7.** 230% **8.** 62.5% **9.** 2140%
10. 123.7% **11.** 117% **12.** 55% **13.** 0.4, $\frac{2}{5}$
14. 0.35, $\frac{7}{20}$ **15.** 0.18, $\frac{9}{50}$ **16.** 1.04, $\frac{26}{25}$

17. 0.5625, $\frac{9}{16}$ **18.** 0.8415, $\frac{1683}{2000}$ **19.** 0.002, $\frac{1}{500}$
20. 1.384, $\frac{173}{125}$ **21.** $\frac{5}{100}$, 0.055, 0.51, 52%, $\frac{11}{20}$
22. $\frac{27}{30}$, 91%, 0.923, $\frac{14}{15}$, 94%, 0.97
23. $\frac{1}{32}$, 3.16%, 0.0328, 0.037, $\frac{4}{105}$
24. 0.742, 75%, $\frac{19}{25}$, $\frac{38}{49}$, $\frac{7}{9}$, 0.788 **25.** white

26. 18% **27.** 43% **28.** 85% **29.** < **30.** > **31.** <
32. = **33.** = **34.** <

Lesson 7.5

1. decrease; 20% **2.** increase; 140%
3. decrease; 8.3% **4.** increase; 1500%
5. increase; 66.7% **6.** decrease; 23.6%
7. 374.5 **8.** 88.3 **9.** 422.5 **10.** 274.3
11. 45,795 **12.** 16,632 **13.** 633.97% **14.** 86.32%
15. 1267.51% **16.** 200% **17.** 150% **18.** 30%
19. 400% **20.** 35.8% **21.** 458.1% **22.** 105.3%
23. 41.6% **24.** 3152.5%

Lesson 7.6

1. \$38.25 **2.** \$27.60 **3.** \$260 **4.** \$47.63
5. \$19.59 **6.** \$79.20 **7.** \$51.41 **8.** \$90.92
9. \$55.58 **10.** \$29.99 **11.** 814% **12.** 27.27%
13. 15% **14.** discount; 15% **15.** markup; 15%
16. discount; 3% **17.** discount; 16%
18. markup; 30% **19.** markup; 80% **20.** \$56.45
21. \$632.15; \$505.72

Lesson 7.7

1. 197.2 **2.** 104.4 **3.** 12 **4.** 1.96 **5.** 390 **6.** 28
7. 297 **8.** 920 **9.** 269% **10.** 11% **11.** 29%
12. 0.3% **13.** \$43.40 **14.** \$86.67 **15.** \$39.38
16. \$400 **17.** \$1111.11
18. $0.20(45) = c$; $\frac{c}{45} = \frac{20}{100}$; 9 credits; yes
19. 9787; 11,895 **20.** = **21.** = **22.** 73,500; 49%

Lesson 7.8

1. $\frac{1}{5}$ **2.** $\frac{2}{25}$ **3.** $\frac{11}{25}$ **4.** $\frac{9}{25}$ **5.** $\frac{8}{25}$ **6.** 0 **7.** $\frac{32}{235}$
8. $\frac{41}{235}$ **9.** $\frac{34}{235}$ **10.** $\frac{111}{235}$ **11.** $\frac{71}{235}$ **12.** 160

A8 **Middle School Math, Course 3**
Practice Workbook

Lesson 7.8 *continued*

13. 32 **14.** 128 **15.** 0 **16.** 85%; 37.5% **17.** $\frac{5}{6}$
18. $\frac{1}{2}$ **19.** 1 **20.** $\frac{5}{6}$ **21.** $\frac{4}{9}$

Lesson 8.1

1. 180° **2.** right **3.** 180° **4.** Complementary
5. Vertical **6.** Right **7.** Parallel
8. supplementary **9.** neither
10. complementary **11.** supplementary **12.** 153°
13. 26° **14.** $m\angle 2 = 83°$, $m\angle 1 = m\angle 3 = 97°$
15. $m\angle 6 = 19°$, $m\angle 5 = m\angle 7 = 161°$ **16.** $m\angle 1 = m\angle 5 = m\angle 7 = 123°$, $m\angle 2 = m\angle 4 = m\angle 6 = m\angle 8 = 57°$ **17.** $x = 22$; $m\angle 1 = 66°$, $m\angle 3 = 114°$ **18.** $x = 12°$; $m\angle 7 = 48°$, $m\angle 8 = 132°$
19. $x = 23°$; $m\angle 5 = 52°$, $m\angle 6 = 52°$

Lesson 8.2

1. obtuse **2.** acute **3.** right **4.** isosceles
5. equilateral **6.** scalene **7.** $x = 74$; acute
8. $x = 43$; obtuse **9.** $x = 48$; right **10.** no; the sum is not 180° **11.** yes; the sum is 180° **12.** yes; the sum is 180° **13.** 23°, 30°, 127° **14.** 81°, 56°, 43° **15.** 90°, 22°, 8° **16.** isosceles triangle
17. right isosceles triangles

Lesson 8.3

1. four **2.** trapezoid **3.** parallel **4.** rhombus
5. right **6.** 4; 4 **7.** rectangle **8.** parallelogram
9. quadrilateral **10.** 94 **11.** 120 **12.** 124
13. 102 **14.** $x = 13$; 60°, 74°, 113°, 113°
15. $x = 9$; 140°, 48°, 137°, 35° **16.** always
17. never **18.** always **19.** sometimes

Lesson 8.4

1. 6 **2.** 7 **3.** 8 **4.** 5 **5.** 12 **6.** n **7.** polygon
8. regular polygon **9.** not a polygon **10.** 144°
11. 160° **12.** 165° **13.** 2160° **14.** $x = 123$
15. $x = 143$ **16.** $x = 89$
17. $x = 50$; $m\angle A = m\angle B = 100°$, $m\angle E = 150°$
18. $x = 114$; $m\angle J = m\angle K = m\angle F = m\angle G = 114°$
19. $x = 60$; $m\angle L = 60°$, $m\angle M = 170°$, $m\angle N = 120°$

20. 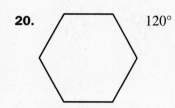 120°

Lesson 8.5

1. $\angle J \cong \angle W$; $\angle K \cong \angle X$; $\angle L \cong \angle Y$; $\angle M \cong \angle Z$
2. $\overline{JM} \cong \overline{WZ}$; $\overline{JK} \cong \overline{WX}$; $\overline{KL} \cong \overline{XY}$; $\overline{LM} \cong \overline{YZ}$
3. $m\angle K = 128°$; $m\angle W = 74°$; $m\angle Z = 68°$
4. 12 in. **5.** 18 in. **6.** $\triangle ABC \cong \triangle WXY$; $\triangle FGH \cong \triangle RST$ **7.** SAS **8.** SSS **9.** SSS; $x - 7 = 6$; $x = 13$ **10.** ASA; $x + 14 = 48$; $x = 34$ **11.** SSS; $x - 15 = 60$; $x = 75$ **12.** no; They are congruent only when they are the same size.

Lesson 8.6

1. no **2.** yes **3.** yes **4.** 4 **5.** 1 **6.** 2
7. $A'(2, 2)$, $B'(2, 5)$, $C'(7, 5)$ **8.** $X'(3, -1)$, $Y'(4, -5)$, $Z'(-2, 3)$

9.
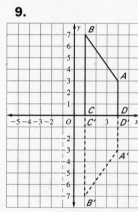

10.
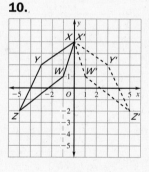

11.
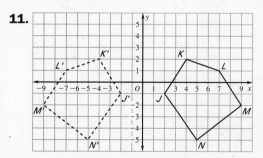

Lesson 8.6 *continued*

12.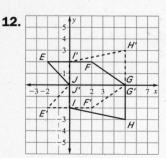

13. *Sample Answers*: A, M **14.** *Sample Answers*:
I, H **15.** 2 **16.** 4 **17.** 1

Lesson 8.7

1. $(x, y) \rightarrow (x - 2, y - 2)$ **2.** $(x, y) \rightarrow$
$(x - 4, y + 1)$ **3.** $(x, y) \rightarrow (x, y + 5)$ **4.** rotation

5. reflection **6.** translation **7.** $X'(-1, 0)$,
$Y'(-6, 3)$, $Z'(-10, -6)$ **8.** $L'(-3, 7)$, $M'(1, 10)$,
$N'(-1, 3)$

9.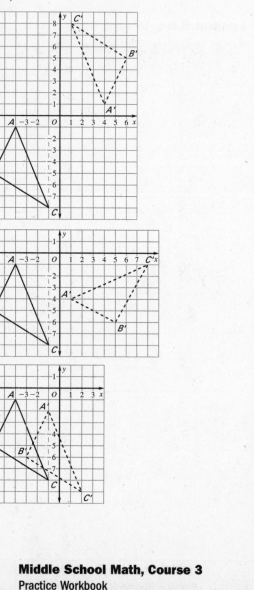

10.

11.

12.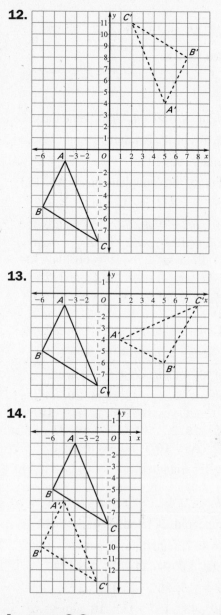

13.

14.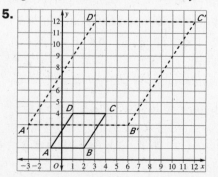

Lesson 8.8

1. *Sample Answer*: rectangle $ABCD \sim$ rectangle
$NQPM$ **2.** *Sample Answer*: triangle $RST \sim$
triangle KJL **3.** 6 ft **4.** $x = 5$ in., $y = 38$

5.

Lesson 8.8 *continued*

6. **7.**

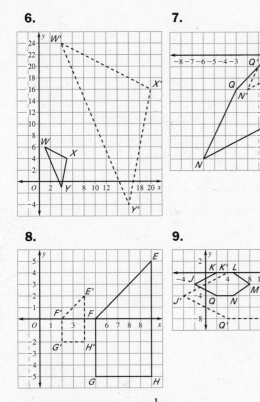

8. **9.**

10. The revised area is $\frac{1}{4}$ the original area.

Lesson 9.1

1. 4 **2.** -6 **3.** 15 **4.** -20 **5.** 4 **6.** 7 **7.** 9

8. 12 **9.** 5.7 **10.** 7.8 **11.** -9.4 **12.** 52.4

13. 57 **14.** 5.2 **15.** 64.9 **16.** -33 **17.** ± 8

18. ± 10 **19.** ± 12 **20.** ± 4 **21.** ± 17 **22.** ± 24

23. ± 5.74 **24.** ± 10.10 **25.** ± 10.86 **26.** ± 16.25

27. ± 15.94 **28.** ± 19.16 **29.** 172 feet **30.** 15

31. 5 **32.** 10 **33.** $-0.8, 0.8$ **34.** $-0.3, 0.3$

35. $-1.3, 1.3$ **36.** $-2.3, 2.3$ **37.** $\frac{1}{3}$ **38.** $\frac{5}{6}$ **39.** $\frac{7}{9}$

40. $\frac{10}{11}$

Lesson 9.2

1. irrational, nonrepeating decimal **2.** rational, repeating decimal **3.** rational, terminating decimal

4. irrational, nonrepeating decimal **5.** irrational, nonrepeating decimal **6.** rational, whole number

7. rational, terminating decimal **8.** rational, repeating decimal **9.** < **10.** = **11.** < **12.** 0.31, $0.3\overline{1}$, $0.\overline{311}$, $0.\overline{31}$, $0.\overline{313}$ **13.** $-0.\overline{94}$, -0.949, $-0.94\overline{4}$, $-0.9\overline{44}$ **14.** $\sqrt{12} \approx 3.46$; irrational

15. 8; rational **16.** 4; rational **17.** $\sqrt{8} \approx 2.83$; irrational **18.** -8.15, -8, $\sqrt{53}$, 7.4 **19.** -3, $\sqrt{64}$,

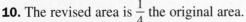

8.2, $\sqrt{137}$ **20.** -4.7, $-\sqrt{21}$, $-\sqrt{\frac{2}{5}}$, $-\frac{5}{9}$

21. $\sqrt{4.8}$, $\frac{12}{5}$, $\sqrt{8.61}$, 3.64 **22.** 18 inches by 18 inches; 96 tiles **23.** 3.51 cm

Lesson 9.3

1. 10 **2.** 18 **3.** 30 **4.** 51 **5.** 35 ft **6.** 20 in.

7. $\frac{3}{5}$ mm **8.** yes **9.** no **10.** no **11.** yes

12. 29.95 m **13.** 26.16 ft **14.** 30.70 in. **15.** yes

16. no **17.** no **18.** yes **19.** 85 in. **20.** 3.5

21. 288 **22.** 44.4 **23.** 1

Lesson 9.4

1. 69.7 ft **2.** 93.9 yd **3.** 291.2 m **4.** 41 ft; 180 ft^2; 90 ft **5.** 24 mm; 216 mm^2; 72 mm

6. 20 in.; 480 in.^{2}; 120 in. **7.** 79.2 yd; 1512 yd^2; 190.2 yd **8.** 146.4 ft; 5355 ft^2; 353.4 ft **9.** 1.5 mm; 0.6 mm^2; 4 mm **10.** yes **11.** no **12.** no **13.** no

14. 120.4 ft **15.** 37.6 m **16.** 30.8 ft **17.** 30.9 in.

18. 15,360 ft^2; 4 bags **19.** 37 in. **20.** 96 m

Lesson 9.5

1. $x = 16\sqrt{2}$ in. **2.** $x = 15$ cm **3.** $x = 24$ ft

4. $x = 16$ in. **5.** $x = 9$ yd; $y = 18$ yd

6. $x = 21.5$ m; $y = 21.5\sqrt{3}$ m **7.** 15 cm

8. 4.08 ft ; 5.77 ft

4.08 ft

9. $x = 11\sqrt{2}$ ft **10.** $x = 11$ mm **11.** $x = 6\sqrt{2}$ in.

12. $x = 21\sqrt{3}$ m; $y = 21$ m **13.** $x = 18$ in.; $y = 9\sqrt{3}$ in. **14.** $x = 37.5$ yd; $y = 37.5\sqrt{3}$ yd

15. $36\sqrt{2}$ m

Lesson 9.6

1. $\sin A = \frac{21}{29}$; $\cos A = \frac{20}{29}$; $\tan A = \frac{21}{20}$;

$\sin B = \frac{20}{29}$; $\cos B = \frac{21}{29}$; $\tan B = \frac{20}{21}$

2. $\sin A = \frac{175}{185}$; $\cos A = \frac{60}{185}$; $\tan A = \frac{175}{60}$;

$\sin B = \frac{60}{185}$; $\cos B = \frac{175}{185}$; $\tan B = \frac{60}{175}$

Lesson 9.6 *continued*

3. $\sin A = \frac{15}{17}$; $\cos A = \frac{8}{17}$; $\tan A = \frac{15}{8}$;

$\sin B = \frac{8}{17}$; $\cos B = \frac{15}{17}$; $\tan B = \frac{8}{15}$

4. 0.3839 **5.** 0.6561 **6.** 0.9925 **7.** 0.5878

8. 9.98 in. **9.** 37.42 ft **10.** 26.65 m **11.** 177.7 m

12. $m\angle G = 62°$; 34 m; $\sin G = \frac{30}{34}$; $\cos G = \frac{16}{34}$;

$\tan G = \frac{30}{16}$ **13.** $m\angle G = 37°$; 32 in.; $\sin G = \frac{24}{40}$;

$\cos G = \frac{32}{40}$; $\tan G = \frac{24}{32}$ **14.** $m\angle G = 46.4°$; 80 yd;

$\sin G = \frac{84}{116}$; $\cos G = \frac{80}{116}$; $\tan G = \frac{84}{80}$

15. 181,481 feet

Lesson 10.1

1. 36 in.^{2} **2.** 77 mm^2 **3.** 91 yd^2 **4.** 99 mm^2

5. 144 in.^{2} **6.** 40 cm^2 **7.** Check student sketch; 23 units **8.** Check student sketch; 7 units

9. Check student sketch; 16 units **10.** 210 cm^2

11. 304 in.^{2} **12.** 168 ft^2 **13.** 10 mm

Lesson 10.2

1. 606.6794 cm^2 **2.** 572.265 yd^2

3. 186.1706 m^2 **4.** 78.5 cm^2 **5.** 530.66 ft^2

6. 4775.94 mm^2 **7.** 200.96 m^2 **8.** 452.16 yd^2

9. 2826 in.^{2} **10.** 3 mm **11.** 5 ft **12.** 9 in.

13. 11 cm **14.** 15 m **15.** 2.4 yd **16.** 314 ft^2

17. 41.7 m **18.** 55.04 m^2 **19.** 72.665 ft^2

20. 25.12 in.^{2} **21.** radius: 8 in.; area: 200.96 in.^{2}

22. radius: 15 m; area: 706.5 m^2 **23.** radius: 24 cm; area: 1808.64 cm^2 **24.** 9 yd **25.** 9.12 in.^{2}

Lesson 10.3

1. rectangular prism; yes

2. octagonal prism; yes **3.** sphere; no

4.

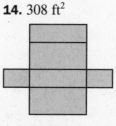

Top   Front   Side

faces: 9; edges: 16; vertices: 9

5.

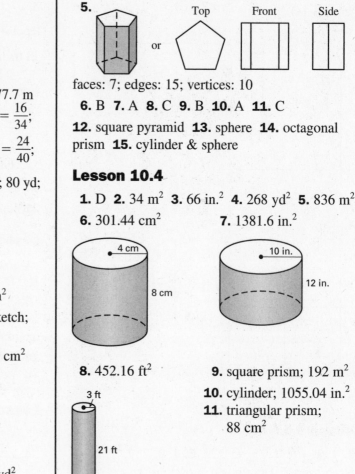

or   Top   Front   Side

faces: 7; edges: 15; vertices: 10

6. B **7.** A **8.** C **9.** B **10.** A **11.** C

12. square pyramid **13.** sphere **14.** octagonal prism **15.** cylinder & sphere

Lesson 10.4

1. D **2.** 34 m^2 **3.** 66 in.^{2} **4.** 268 yd^2 **5.** 836 m^2

6. 301.44 cm^2 **7.** 1381.6 in.^{2}

4 cm   8 cm   10 in.   12 in.

8. 452.16 ft^2 **9.** square prism; 192 m^2

10. cylinder; 1055.04 in.^{2}

3 ft   21 ft   **11.** triangular prism; 88 cm^2

12. 100.48 in.^{2} **13.** 240 m^2

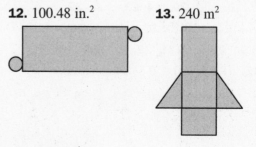

14. 308 ft^2

15. 2549.68 m^2 **16.** 752 in.^{2} **17.** 504 cm^2

Lesson 10.5

1. 120 m² **2.** 304 in.² **3.** 501.6 cm²
4. 831.6 yd² **5.** 282.6 m² **6.** 785 in.²
7. 922.532 cm² **8.** 2426.592 yd²
9. 565.5 cm² **10.** 1658.8 in.²

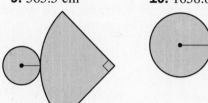

11. 179 yd²

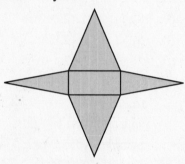

12. 552 in.² **13.** 24.5 mm² **14.** 3880.5 in.²
15. 56 m² **16.** 395.8 in.² **17.** 81 yd²

Lesson 10.6

1. 360 m³ **2.** 2100 in.³ **3.** 701.76 yd³
4. 510 mm³ **5.** 1356.48 in.³ **6.** 163.28 cm³
7. 98.61798 m³ **8.** 364 mm³ **9.** 1055.58 ft³
10. 5176.5 m³ **11.** 17,280 mm³
12. 244.49 in.³ **13.** 138.528 in.³ **14.** 680 cm³
15. 3397.42 ft³ **16.** 3763.75 in.³

Lesson 10.7

1. 30 in.³ **2.** 6.09 mm³ **3.** 36.4 cm³ **4.** 320 in.³
5. 110 m³ **6.** 21 in.³ **7.** 378 mm³ **8.** 13.5 ft³
9. 1272.3 in.³ **10.** 29,914.2 mm³ **11.** 2375.0 ft³
12. 201.1 in.³ **13.** 3,879,238.6 cm³ **14.** 760.3 ft³
15. 1.3 in.³ **16.** 289 m³

Lesson 11.1

1. input; output **2.** one **3.** domain **4.** range
5. domain; range **6.** no **7.** no **8.** yes **9.** no

10.

Input x	−2	−1	0	1	2
Output y	−5	−3	−1	1	3

range: all real numbers

11.

Input x	−2	−1	0	1	2
Output y	7	4	3	4	7

range: all real numbers greater than or equal to 3

12.

Input x	−2	−1	0	1	2
Output y	$\frac{1}{2}$	$\frac{3}{4}$	1	$1\frac{1}{4}$	$1\frac{1}{2}$

range: all real numbers

13.

Input x	−2	−1	0	1	2
Output y	−1	−4	−7	−10	−13

range: all real numbers **14.** $y = 5x + 2$

15. $y = x + 1$ **16.** Yes; for every input (number of meals ordered) you get a different output (price).

17. no **18.** $t = 14r − 3$ **19.** $t = 8r + 4$

Lesson 11.2

1. scatter **2.** increase; increase **3.** decrease; increase **4.** pattern

5.

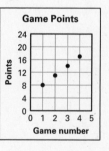

As you play more games, you score more points per game.

6.

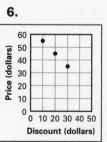

7.

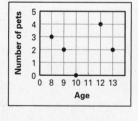

As the discount goes up, the price goes down.

no relationship

Lesson 11.2 *continued*

8.

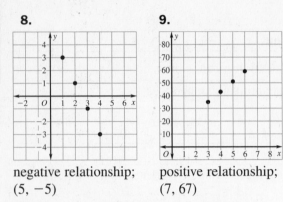

9.

negative relationship;
$(5, -5)$

positive relationship;
$(7, 67)$

10. no relationship **11.** positive relationship

12. negative relationship

13.

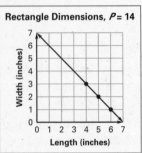

Rectangle Dimensions, $P = 14$

When length = 4.5 in., width = 2.5 in.

Lesson 11.3

1.

x	-7	0	7	14
y	4	11	18	25

2.

x	-7	0	7	14
y	34	13	-8	-29

3.

x	-7	0	7	14
y	-1	-15	-29	-43

4. no **5.** no **6.** yes **7.** no **8.** yes **9.** yes

10. *Sample Answer:* $(0, 6), (1, 8), (2, 10), (-1, 4)$

11. *Sample Answer:* $(0, -5), (1, -9), (2, -13),$
$(-1, -1)$ **12.** *Sample Answer:* $(0, 3), (2, 4),$
$(4, 5), (-2, 2)$ **13.** *Sample Answer:* $(0, 24), (1, 17),$
$(2, 10), (-1, 31)$ **14.** *Sample Answer:* $(0, 1), (8, 6),$
$(16, 11), (-8, -4)$ **15.** *Sample Answer:* $(0, -8),$
$(3, -7), (6, -6), (-3, -9)$ **16.** no **17.** yes

18. yes **19.** no **20.** 10 **21.** $y = 3x + 1$

22. $y = 5 - 3x$

23. $4 \times 1 + 12 \times (-1) = 4 + (-12) = -8 \neq 15$

Lesson 11.4

1. A **2.** B **3.** C

4. *Sample Answer:*

x	0	1	2	3
y	-7	-4	-1	2

5. *Sample Answer:*

x	0	1	2	3
y	4	4	4	4

6. *Sample Answer:*

x	0	1	2	3
y	1.8	2.2	2.6	3

7. *Sample Answer:* $(0, -8), (1, -9), (2, -10)$

8. *Sample Answer:* $(0, -5), (1, -1), (2, 3)$

9. *Sample Answer:* $(0, -3), (1, -3), (2, -3)$

10. yes **11.** yes **12.** no

13.

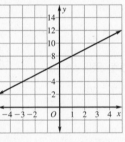

14.

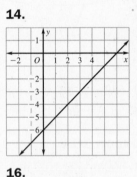

15.

16.

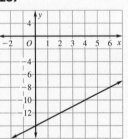

17.

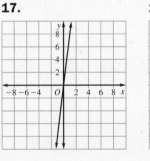

18.

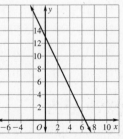

Lesson 11.4 *continued*

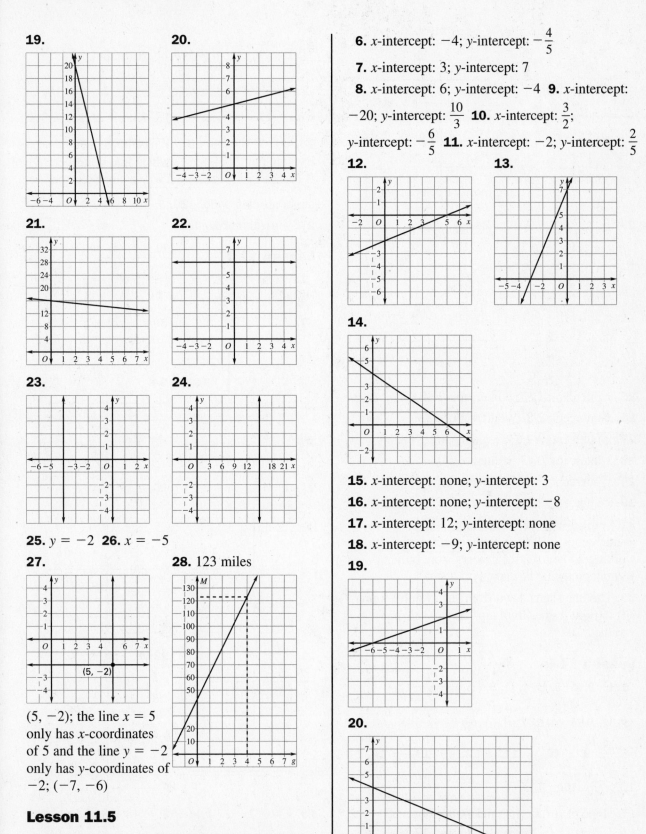

19.

20.

21.

22.

23.

24.

25. $y = -2$ **26.** $x = -5$

27.

28. 123 miles

$(5, -2)$; the line $x = 5$ only has x-coordinates of 5 and the line $y = -2$ only has y-coordinates of -2; $(-7, -6)$

Lesson 11.5

1. x-intercept: -3; y-intercept: 5 **2.** x-intercept: -3; y-intercept: -5 **3.** x-intercept: 2; y-intercept: -6 **4.** x-intercept: 4; y-intercept: 16

5. x-intercept: -3; y-intercept: 27

6. x-intercept: -4; y-intercept: $-\dfrac{4}{5}$

7. x-intercept: 3; y-intercept: 7

8. x-intercept: 6; y-intercept: -4 **9.** x-intercept: -20; y-intercept: $\dfrac{10}{3}$ **10.** x-intercept: $\dfrac{3}{2}$; y-intercept: $-\dfrac{6}{5}$ **11.** x-intercept: -2; y-intercept: $\dfrac{2}{5}$

12.

13.

14.

15. x-intercept: none; y-intercept: 3

16. x-intercept: none; y-intercept: -8

17. x-intercept: 12; y-intercept: none

18. x-intercept: -9; y-intercept: none

19.

20.

Lesson 11.5 *continued*

21. **22.**

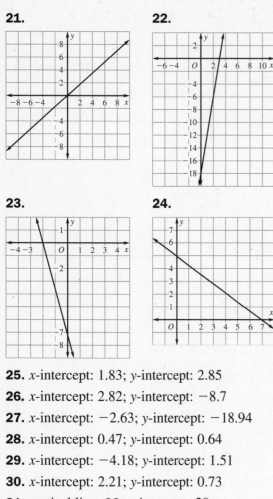

23. **24.**

25. *x*-intercept: 1.83; *y*-intercept: 2.85

26. *x*-intercept: 2.82; *y*-intercept: −8.7

27. *x*-intercept: −2.63; *y*-intercept: −18.94

28. *x*-intercept: 0.47; *y*-intercept: 0.64

29. *x*-intercept: −4.18; *y*-intercept: 1.51

30. *x*-intercept: 2.21; *y*-intercept: 0.73

31. vertical line **32.** *g*-intercept: 20;
m-intercept: 16; Peyton could earn the $240 by
working 20 hours at the grocery store only, or
16 hours mowing lawns only.

33. The line slants down from left to right; from
left to right it goes from a positive *y*-value to a
y-value of 0.

Lesson 11.6

1. C **2.** A **3.** B **4.** D **5.** $(3, 0), (0, -7)$; $\frac{7}{3}$

6. $(2, 6), (-3, 6)$; 0 **7.** $(1, 4), (-4, -2)$; $\frac{6}{5}$

8. $\frac{9}{10}$ **9.** 3 **10.** $\frac{7}{11}$ **11.** $\frac{8}{5}$ **12.** −1 **13.** $\frac{9}{17}$ **14.** 2

15. $-\frac{23}{28}$ **16.** $-1\frac{11}{17}$

17. slope of $\overline{AB}$: 0; $\overline{AC}$: undefined; slope of

$\overline{BC}$: −2 **18.** slope of $\overline{EF}$: $-\frac{8}{5}$; slope of $\overline{FG}$: $\frac{3}{5}$;

slope of $\overline{GE}$: $-\frac{1}{2}$ **19.** slope of $\overline{LM}$: $-\frac{7}{3}$; slope of

$\overline{MN}$: $-\frac{4}{3}$; slope of $\overline{NL}$: $-\frac{11}{6}$ **20.** slope of $\overline{XY}$: $\frac{3}{8}$;

slope of $\overline{YZ}$: $-\frac{2}{5}$; slope of $\overline{ZX}$: $-\frac{7}{2}$ **21.** $x = 16$;

$y = \frac{3}{4}$ **22.** $x = 4$; $y = -13$ **23.** $x = 0$; $y = -3$

24. $x = 7$; $y = 26$ **25.** $\overline{XY}$ has the greater slope;
By graphing: look to see which line is steeper;
By calculating: determine which slope has the
larger absolute value **26.** $-\frac{4}{3}$

27. vertical; horizontal

Lesson 11.7

1. $y = 5x - 8$ **2.** $y = 11x + 13$ **3.** $y = -\frac{7}{2}x + 6$

4. C **5.** A **6.** B

7. *m:* 1; *b:* 9 **8.** *m:* $\frac{1}{5}$; *b:* −2

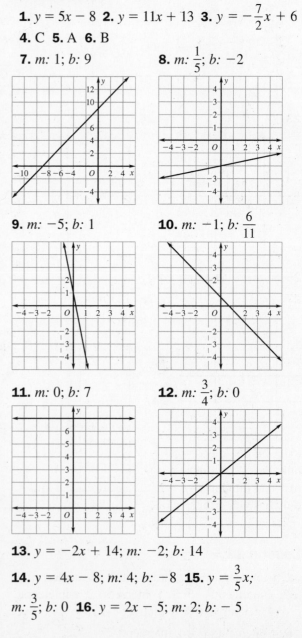

9. *m:* −5; *b:* 1 **10.** *m:* −1; *b:* $\frac{6}{11}$

11. *m:* 0; *b:* 7 **12.** *m:* $\frac{3}{4}$; *b:* 0

13. $y = -2x + 14$; *m:* −2; *b:* 14

14. $y = 4x - 8$; *m:* 4; *b:* −8 **15.** $y = \frac{3}{5}x$;

m: $\frac{3}{5}$; *b:* 0 **16.** $y = 2x - 5$; *m:* 2; *b:* −5

Lesson 11.7 *continued*

17. $y = \frac{1}{8}x - 7$; m: $\frac{1}{8}$; b: -7 **18.** $y = 1.5x - 3.2$; m: 1.5; b: -3.2 **19.** $y = -\frac{3}{4}x + 7$

20. $y = 5x - 4$

Lesson 11.8

1. no **2.** yes **3.** yes **4.** no **5.** C **6.** D **7.** A **8.** B

9.

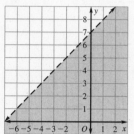

10.

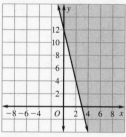

11.

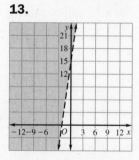

12.

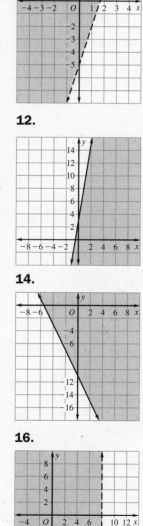

13.

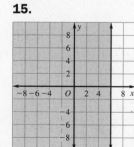

14.

15.

16.

17.

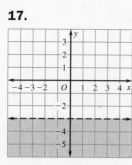

18.

19.

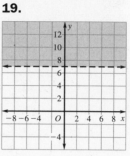

20.

21. up to 9 sandwiches

22.

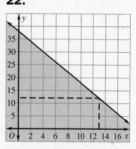

23. 12 **24.** $4x + 2y < 5$

25. *Sample Answer*: $3x - y < 2$

Lesson 12.1

1.
```
4 | 0 2
5 | 3
6 | 1 5 8
7 | 2
8 |
9 | 3
```
Key: 6 | 5 = 65; 60–69

2.
```
0 | 5 6 8
1 | 5 9
2 | 2 7
3 | 3 7
```
Key: 2 | 7 = 27; 0–9

3.
```
12 | 2 4 9
13 | 5
14 | 8
15 | 2
16 | 8
```
Key: 14 | 8 = 148; 120–129

4.
```
30 | 1 6 9
31 | 6
32 | 2 5 7
33 | 5
34 | 8
```
Key: 32 | 5 = 325; 300–309, 320–329

Lesson 12.1 *continued*

5.
20	1
21	3 7 9
22	
23	4 8
24	
25	
26	3

Key: 23 | 4 = 23.4;
21.0–21.9

6.
4	1
5	
6	8
7	3
8	4 5
9	2 3 7
10	3

Key: 8 | 4 = 8.4;
9.0–9.9

7. 50; 23; 50–59

8.
0	8
1	3 5 6 9
2	4 6 6 9
3	3 4 7 8
4	5

Key: 2 | 6 = 26; 37; more

9.
Set A		Set B
	1	9
6	2	3 4 6 9
9 5 4 1	3	5 8
8	4	1
6	5	

1 | 3 | 5 represents
31 and 35.

10.
Set C		Set D
6 3 2	5	
2	6	2 3 3 8 9
2	7	1 4
1	8	2
2	9	

1 | 8 | 2 represents
81 and 82.

11.
SUV		Sedan
9 7 6	1	
2 1	2	3 4 8
	3	0 1

1 | 2 | 3 represents 21 and 30; sedans have a higher
median mpg than SUVs.

12.
6	0 5
7	3 6
8	1 5
9	2 2

Key: 7 | 6 = 76; 32

13. 152, 185, 216, 165, 234, 206, 193, 234

14.
15	2
16	5
17	
18	5
19	3
20	6
21	6
22	
23	4 4

Key: 19 | 3 = 193
Sample Answer: numbers are
higher, range is greater

Lesson 12.2

1. lower; upper

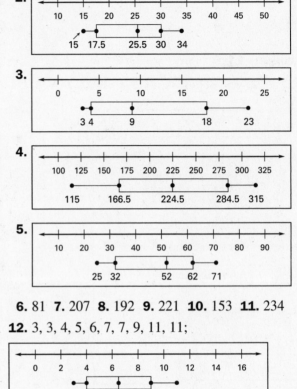

2.
3.
4.
5.

6. 81 **7.** 207 **8.** 192 **9.** 221 **10.** 153 **11.** 234

12. 3, 3, 4, 5, 6, 7, 7, 9, 11, 11;

Sample Answer: She averages about 7 miles a day.

13.

Sample Answer: Median mass of an Indian
elephant is 3212 kilograms. **14.** Player B averages
more goals per game. Player B is more consistent
because the range is smaller.

Lesson 12.3

1. 90° **2.** 135° **3.** 144° **4.** 64.8°

Lesson 12.3 *continued*

5.

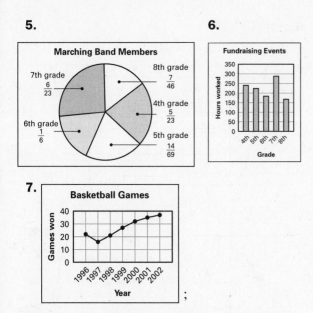

6.

7.

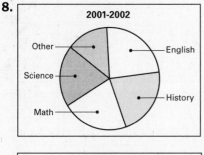

;

As time goes on, the number of wins increases.

8.

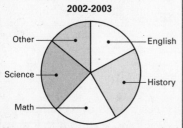

9. Science, English

10. bar graph; *Sample Answer:* Data will be displayed in distinct categories.

11. line graph; *Sample Answer:* Data will be displayed over time.

Lesson 12.4

1. 6 **2.** 6 **3.** 8 **4.** 9 **5.** $\frac{1}{243}$ **6.** See student diagram; 24 options **7.** 30,000 **8.** $\frac{1}{10}$ **9.** $\frac{1}{27}$ **10.** $\frac{1}{32}$

Lesson 12.5

1. 7; 6; 5; 4; 3; 2; 1 **2.** 7; 3 **3.** D **4.** B **5.** C

6. A **7.** 5040 **8.** 3,628,800 **9.** 40,320

10. 1 **11.** 3 **12.** 210 **13.** 181,440 **14.** 120

15. 6,652,800 **16.** 32,760 **17.** 13,366,080

18. 420 **19.** 3360 **20.** 720

21. $10 \times 10 \times 10 \times 10$; $10 \times 9 \times 8 \times 7$

22. No; $_6P_4 = \dfrac{6!}{(6-4)!}$ **23.** 42 **24.** 362,880

Lesson 12.6

1. 10 **2.** 20 **3.** 36 **4.** 495 **5.** 70 **6.** 210 **7.** 330

8. 5005 **9.** 7 **10.** 171 **11.** 5,200,300 **12.** 3321

13. 98,280 **14.** 1820 **15.** 10 **16.** 56 **17.** 792

18. 153; 816 **19.** combination; 28

20. permutation; 362,880 **21.** combination; 495

22. combination; 1001

Lesson 12.7

1. 27% **2.** $\frac{2}{5}$ **3.** 0.59 **4.** $\frac{1}{13}$ **5.** $\frac{1}{11}$; $\frac{1}{10}$ **6.** $\frac{2}{11}$; $\frac{2}{9}$

7. 0; $\frac{0}{11}$ **8.** $\frac{2}{3}$ **9.** $\frac{1}{2}$ **10.** $\frac{1}{5}$ **11.** 0 **12.** $\frac{5}{1}$ **13.** $\frac{24}{13}$

14. $\frac{1}{2}$ **15.** $\frac{3}{8}$ **16.** $\frac{3}{8}$ **17.** $\frac{1}{8}$ **18.** $\frac{23}{100} = 0.23$ **19.** $\frac{6}{19}$

20. $\frac{23}{2}$

Lesson 12.8

1. 0.3 **2.** 0.9 **3.** 0.5 **4.** 0.248 **5.** 1 **6.** 0.45

7. independent; 0.0278 **8.** dependent; 0.0659

9. independent; 0.25 **10.** $\frac{1}{27}$ **11.** 0.03125; 0.25

12. 0.000001

Lesson 13.1

1. trinomial **2.** polynomial **3.** binomial

4. monomial **5.** $3m^2 - m + 9$

6. $-9w^4 + 8w + 13$ **7.** $5b^5 - 4b^3 - 2b + 8$

8. $2x + 14$ **9.** $5x^3 + 2x^2 + x$

10. $2m^3 - 2m^2 + 7m$ **11.** $6d^2 - 18d + 11$

12. $5c^7 + 6c^5 - 3c$ **13.** $4w^6 - 3w^4 + 17$

14. $x^2 + 13x + 3$ **15.** $12x - 24$

16. $-4c^3 + 5c^2 + 9c - 3$

17. $9m^3 + 5m^2 - 2m + 15$ **18.** $-18w^3 + 36w^2$

19. $-24x^2 - 9x - 3$ **20.** 1088 ft **21.** 1059 ft

Lesson 13.1 *continued*

22. 780 ft **23.** 90.5 ft **24.** $-5x^2 + 4x$
25. $-4x^2 + 25x - 81$

Lesson 13.2

1. $-4x + 11$ **2.** $-2x + 2$ **3.** $9x - 5$
4. $10x^2 + 9x$ **5.** $-2x^2 + 4x + 4$
6. $15x^2 - 11x - 29$ **7.** $6x - 7$ **8.** $-14x + 7$
9. $-3x^2 + 11x$ **10.** $9x^2 + 4x - 30$
11. $5x^2 + 8x - 1$ **12.** $-4x^3 - 12x^2 - 12x + 19$
13. $17x + 4$ **14.** $36x - 4$ **15.** $7c^3 - 12c^2 - 2c$
16. $-13k^3 + 5k^2 + 19k - 28$ **17.** $8w + 4$
18. $-14d + 13$ **19.** $25x^2; 13x^2 - 2$
20. $-8x + 14$ **21.** $11x^2 - 8x + 13$
22. $33x^2 - 12x$ **23.** $9x^3 - 17x^2 + 13x - 14$

Lesson 13.3

1. $-15x^5$ **2.** $72x^8$ **3.** $6x^6$ **4.** $-60b^{10}$ **5.** w^{11}
6. $-q^{17}$ **7.** $t^2 - 7t$ **8.** $7m^2 + 21m$ **9.** $-k^3 + 6k$
10. $-9x^6 + 9x^2$ **11.** $-4a^3 + 15a^2$
12. $96p - 12p^4$ **13.** $64x^3$ **14.** $a^4b^4c^4$ **15.** $32x^5y^5$
16. $9q^2$ **17.** $-c^7d^7$ **18.** $125m^3n^3$ **19.** $46,656r^6s^6$
20. $6561e^4f^4$ **21.** x^{15} **22.** a^{24} **23.** b^{14} **24.** e^{45}
25. b^4g^{12} **26.** $k^{12}l^{30}$ **27.** $9p^8$ **28.** $64u^{21}$
29. $192a^3b^{15}$ **30.** $-5x^{17}y^2z^6$ **31.** $-6m^7n^7p$
32. 5.764801×10^{30} **33.** 8.1×10^{37}
34. 3.2768×10^{44} **35.** 5.11×10^{14} m^2
36. 6.42×10^{16} m^2 **37.** 126

Lesson 13.4

1. C **2.** A **3.** D **4.** B **5.** $x^2 - 4x - 21$
6. $x^2 + 13x + 36$ **7.** $x^2 - 18x + 72$
8. $2m^2 - 5m - 12$ **9.** $5a^2 - 38a + 48$
10. $-9p^2 - 14p + 39$ **11.** $7f^2 - 36f + 32$
12. $45w^2 - 28w - 33$ **13.** $24b^2 - 30b - 21$
14. $x^2 + 9x - 36$ **15.** $x^2 - 7x - 30$
16. $x^4 - 11x^2 + 28$ **17.** $25x^2 + 5x - 12$
18. $24x^2 - 48x - 30$ **19.** $(x - 4)^2 = x^2 - 8x + 16$;
$x^2 + 16$ is missing the middle term **20.** $x + 2$
21. $25(r^3 + 3r^2 + 3r + 1)$; $29.78

Lesson 13.5

1. $f(x) = 5x^2$ **2.** $f(x) = -3x^2 - 6$
3. $f(x) = -7x^2$ **4.** 28, 0, 28 **5.** 2, -6, 2

6. $-16, 0, -16$
7. $f(x) = 8.5x^2 + 4150$; 10 years

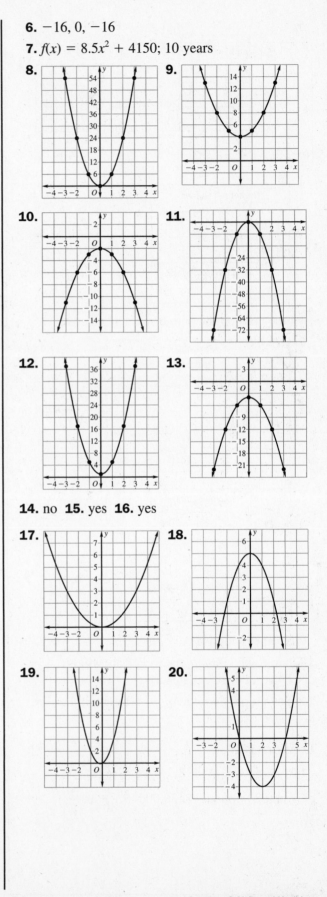

14. no **15.** yes **16.** yes

21.

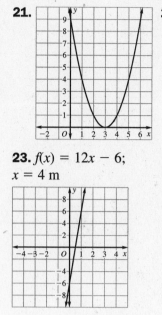

22.

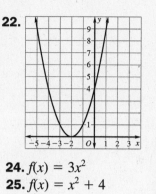

23. $f(x) = 12x - 6;$
$x = 4$ m

24. $f(x) = 3x^2$

25. $f(x) = x^2 + 4$